Trust Rules

Trust Rules

How to Tell the Good Guys
from the Bad Guys
in Work and Life

Second Edition

Linda K. Stroh, PhD

Foreword by Faye J. Crosby, PhD

 PRAEGER ™

An Imprint of ABC-CLIO, LLC
Santa Barbara, California • Denver, Colorado

Library of Congress Cataloging-in-Publication Data

Stroh, Linda K.
    Trust rules : how to tell the good guys from the bad guys in work and life / Linda K.
Stroh ; foreword by Faye J. Crosby. — Second edition.
        pages cm
    Includes bibliographical references.
    ISBN 978-1-4408-4064-7 (hardback) — ISBN 978-1-4408-4065-4
(e-book)   1. Organizational behavior.   2. Trust.   3. Interpersonal relations.
4. Work environment.   I. Title.
    HD58.7.S775 2015
    650.1'3—dc23   2015021410

ISBN: 978-1-4408-4064-7
EISBN: 978-1-4408-4065-4

19 18 17 16 15   1 2 3 4 5

This book is also available on the World Wide Web as an eBook.
Visit www.abc-clio.com for details.

Praeger
An Imprint of ABC-CLIO, LLC

ABC-CLIO, LLC
130 Cremona Drive, P.O. Box 1911
Santa Barbara, California 93116-1911

This book is printed on acid-free paper ∞
Manufactured in the United States of America

*It is because of Greg, Angie, Joe, Brad, Brandy, Brayden, and Brooke
that I wake up every day of my life wanting to learn how
to be a better guy. This book is dedicated to them. I know
they know how much I love every one of them!*

Contents

viii   *Contents*

Foreword

WE ALL KNOW THE importance of trust. But few of us are really skilled at identifying who is trustworthy and who is not. And many of us wish that we could trust others and even ourselves more than we do.

Trust Rules is an extraordinary book. It is written in a straightforward style that makes the concepts easy to understand, and it includes vignettes and quotations that bring those concepts to life. Free of jargon, the book allows readers from all walks of life to gain insight into a simple and powerful truth: If you can surround yourself with people you trust, your life will be immeasurably sweeter than otherwise.

"Well, of course," you say, "but how can I surround myself with people who deserve my trust? Such a luxury is beyond my control." So think many of us. We don't realize how to develop and exercise our own powers; we don't recognize how we can attach ourselves to people we can trust and how we can free our lives of people we cannot trust.

A careful reading of *Trust Rules*, with its plain-speaking, level-headed prose, will let you learn how to take the steps toward creating a life at work and a life at home in which you can form alliances and attachments to those you can trust and avoid the others. This book tells you how to differentiate between those who are trustworthy and those who are not.

This accessible monograph also opens the reflective reader to a new understanding about the connection between two related concepts: (1) being trusting, and (2) being trustworthy. Naïvely, we may think that being trusting and being trustworthy are just two sides of the same coin. In fact, trustworthy people may not be particularly trusting. Instead, those who are most trustworthy are the ones who have identified those whom they should distrust and thus avoid. When you know whom to trust and whom to distrust, you can become more trustworthy yourself, which in turn allows you to know better whom to trust. And the cycle continues.

And what if a trusted colleague, friend, or loved one breaks our trust? Again, *Trust Rules* offers advice that is both profound and practical. It provides you with the means to assess whether the culprit has learned from his or her mistakes.

Leaders come in all varieties. Some leaders have a need for power. They like to assert dominance over others. Such leaders get their way through punishments and threats. Some leaders rely less on dominance than on manipulation. Such leaders get their way through rewards and incentives. And some leaders—inspirational leaders—care less about controlling or manipulating the behavior of others and care more about empowering others. Such leaders are great teachers and guides.

Linda Stroh devotes her life to the empowerment of others. In her interactions with others, Dr. Stroh finds points of common contact and uses these to help others find their own true paths. From my first-hand knowledge of Dr. Stroh's work as a professor, as a researcher, and as a consultant, I know that she is an inspirational leader. She is a great guide and a great teacher.

Marking the culmination of years of research and reflection, *Trust Rules* is an empowering book. It is a book that can be read and re-read. With each re-reading new truths become apparent to the reader. That has been my experience, and it has been the experience of many business leaders. It has also been so for the students in my college, Cowell College at the University of California Santa Cruz.

Reading this book and stopping to think about its insights and messages, you will come to know much about the rules of trust—how they operate in the world of work and the world at home. Knowing those rules, you will have within your grasp the means of creating for yourself a world in which, with happiness and fulfillment, trust rules.

Faye J. Crosby, PhD
Provost, Cowell College
Distinguished Professor of Psychology
University of California, Santa Cruz

Acknowledgments

A NYONE LOOKING FOR a great editor should reach out to Karen K. Brees, PhD (karenbrees@gmail.com). Karen is unbelievably talented, and provides phenomenal feedback, editing, and ideas. She gently critiques my writing (even when it's horrible) and makes me laugh at my mistakes. I can't wait to work with Karen again.

A special thanks to Dr. Faye Crosby for writing the foreword for this book. She's the busiest *best guy* I know, yet took time to write this wonderful foreword. She's a treasured friend and colleague. Thanks, Faye!

Thanks to Greg, Angie, Joe, Brad, and Brandy for reviewing several chapters of this book. Their feedback was immeasurable.

Thanks also to Amanda Stevens for her research skills and contributions to some new ideas for the book.

And, thanks to my friend, Ron Elliott, for his wise and thoughtful comments on several chapters in this book. He's a busy *good guy* and I thank him for taking time to do so.

Thanks to you, Hilary Claggett, for guiding me through the Praeger rules and regulations of publishing this book.

Thanks also to all of the people I interviewed for this book. And thanks as well to my parents, brothers, sisters, and especially those whose words I quoted and ideas I have used to write this book.

All of these people have touched my life in meaningful ways . . . I'm indebted to you all.

Introduction

Few delights can equal the mere presence of one whom we trust utterly.

—George MacDonald

I'VE BEEN TEACHING a class about how to *tell the good guys from the bad guys in work and life* at the University of California Santa Cruz (UCSC). It's all about figuring out whom we can and can't trust in our work and personal lives. From this classroom experience and the hundreds of interviews I've undertaken, I've seen firsthand how grappling with trust issues is something that most of us deal with in very haphazard ways. We often don't think about trust until it's too late—until someone has betrayed us or disappointed us, often in very egregious ways.

It's clear that the students in my class are hungry to learn how to do a better job of assessing trustworthy people. Some of them have been betrayed by friends, neighbors, work associates, and worse yet, family members. Others just want to learn to become more trustworthy themselves; and some just need two credits for the quarter, and the time slot works perfectly for them!

Regardless, the students all come away from the course thinking differently about trust than they did before. Most of them say that while they may have taken the course to learn who is and who is not trustworthy, the most important thing they learn is how to become more trustworthy themselves. I hope the same will be true for you while reading this book—you'll be better able to know whom you can and can't trust, and you will also discover how to become more trustworthy yourself. That's what happened for me, too! I started out trying to figure out whom I could and couldn't trust and realized I had a bit of work to do on myself, too!

Did you ever ask yourself what trust means to you? How would you define trust in your life? Give it a try—whom do you REALLY trust in your personal life? Take a moment—think about why you trust them.

Whom do you REALLY trust in your work life? Why do you trust them?

I know there are many people out there, just like me, who have a hard time telling the good guys from the bad guys at work, in social situations, and in other areas of life. For me, sorting the good guys from the bad guys is all about figuring out whom I can (and can't) trust. It's also about finding happiness in my work and personal relationships. Whatever your occupation—President of the United States, CEO of a major multinational company, factory worker, schoolteacher, service industry worker, stay-at-home mom or dad, whatever— the fact remains that there is nothing more valuable in your life than sharing it with people you know you can trust (in both the workplace and your home). This book explores the territory of trust in the workplace and life while also giving some helpful hints about how to choose more trustworthy people with whom to surround ourselves.

When we have trust in those around us, all parts of our lives become more balanced, making our lives much easier to manage. When a spouse or partner is honest and trustworthy, we can better cope with the challenges of couple- dom and have a greater chance of an extraordinary partnership. When I trust that my coworkers and my boss have my best interests at heart—they do what they say and say what they do—then life is far less complicated and more joy- ful. Living and working with people we trust makes life more fun, productive, and rewarding. Most importantly, having trusted confidants in our lives gives us a sense of peace that's without a price tag. As the well-known truism goes: having trust in our lives—priceless.

Before we begin, let me share three of my core beliefs with you.

1. It's better to be a good guy than a bad guy. It's better to be a trustwor- thy person than not.

2. Trusting too much is just as detrimental to our welfare as not trust- ing enough.

3. Those in our inner circles at work, in life, and in social situations have significant influences on our thinking and our behavior. Con- sequently, we must take great care when deciding whom we will and will not let into our inner circles of confidants.

THE FLIP SIDE

There's a flip side to the *good guy–bad guy* equation. If relationships don't meet the standard of trustworthiness, we can suffer the negative effects of working with, living with, or otherwise sharing time with people we can't trust.

In economic terms, the opportunity cost of not trusting—in wasted time, money, mental energy, and physical and emotional health—is immense. Instead of enjoying life, we focus on protecting ourselves from negative influences— *bad guys*—who might lie or cheat to gain something that is ours: resources, money, time, friendships, or, most of all, our peace of mind.

It seems obvious now, but for perhaps the first time, I've realized how my life has been influenced by the people I chose to let into my inner circle. Some were great choices, others were not so great. Regardless, I've learned from them all.

I must have known this early on, but today this notion takes on new meaning for me. You know that moment when the light bulb in your head goes on and you finally understand something more clearly than ever before? That's what's happened for me. I now have greater clarity about how important an inner circle of confidants is to the people that we become. I know it from my own life. I know it from the lives I've observed—my spouse, children, family, friends, and coworkers—and I know it from the academic and applied research I've done.

Thus, this book focuses on how to select a *trusted inner circle*—one that may or may not include the friends, family, or coworkers that seem to be there today.

An inner circle is composed of people we would pretty darn near trust with our lives, or our kids' lives (if we have them)! We trust those in our inner circle to provide support for the good in us. They reinforce our positive behaviors in ways that encourage us to be people of integrity. If our inner circle is made up of bad guys, however, we're in trouble. By not criticizing our poor behaviors, or doing so in ways that aren't effective, or ignoring our bad behavior, or worse yet, supporting those bad behaviors, they show us that it's okay to be a bad guy.

A SIMPLE LESSON?

It looks to be a very simple lesson. Choose good guys (those who are trustworthy) for that all-important inner circle. When we do, we'll discover that our lives will be enriched. We'll have greater peace of mind. We'll have less stress, and some would even argue, as you will see in later chapters, our lives will be longer and healthier.

Unfortunately, it's not really that simple. If it were, the issue of trust wouldn't receive so much attention and play such a critical role in our personal and professional lives. Researchers and philosophers—Socrates, Plato, Aristotle, Confucius, Kant, Dilbert, Lucy and Charlie Brown (to name a few)—have examined the issue of trust, but there has never been a systematic study that examines how people make decisions about whom they let into their inner circle of confidants. This book seeks to fill that gap.

I begin this book with a discussion about trust and its importance to our work and personal lives. Together, we'll take a unique look at the characteristics of a trusting relationship. Then we'll consider the decision-making process that's involved in granting admission to our inner circle. In this new edition, I've added a chapter about *Telling the Truth about Telling the Truth*, where we will learn the negative mental and physical aspects of telling lies. I've also added a chapter about how we can better manage our emotions, thus allowing us to become better guys ourselves. There's another new chapter that helps us build more trusting relationships in our families and one that explores the important concept of leadership and trust. We'll also examine forgiveness and the factors that influence our willingness to forgive. We'll consider important factors for working with untrustworthy people and the ways in which we allow ourselves to be fooled by bad guys. We'll look at how to cope when we've been betrayed and are considering reconciling with someone who has betrayed us. Also new to this book, we'll take a look at how trust works in the world of the Internet. We'll more closely examine our own trustworthiness and find ways we can become better guys to ourselves and others. We'll ultimately discover who can and can't be trusted to be our most valued colleagues, friends, and/or life partners—we'll learn how to tell the good guys from the bad guys in work and life.

SOME BACKGROUND

I grew up in a family where trust was taken for granted. Lying, cheating, stealing, and not following through on promises were never options. Life was far from perfect, but my family members provided each other with unconditional support and encouragement. This wasn't an ostentatious kind of support, but an understated sense that someone was always in my corner.

As with most things in life, there was a downside to growing up with people I could count on and trust. I was slow to learn that not everyone is worthy of trust. And, more importantly, I was slow to learn how to distinguish those I could trust from those I couldn't. The distinctions between the good guys and the bad guys are not always obvious: It's easy to distinguish Luke Skywalker from Darth Vader; it's easy to distinguish the Dalai Lama from Osama Bin Laden. For the most part, however, separating the good guys from the bad guys is much more complicated. Clear distinctions aren't so easy to make, and sometimes people's behaviors can shift situationally or across time, making it even harder to decide.

That's what this book is about—helping us learn how to separate the good guys from the bad guys at work and in our personal lives.

I BEGAN TO WONDER . . .

Although being a trusting person has served me well in most of my work and social interactions, some situations haven't always gone as expected. When I observe people living with untrusting situations at work, home, or in their social lives, or when I've found myself in those same situations, I see how much valuable time is wasted, worrying about what might happen to us, bracing for the inevitable, or trying to emotionally recover from something the untrustworthy person has done.

I began to wonder. Could I become better at distinguishing the good guys from the bad guys? Could I become better at dealing with the bad guys when I am forced to interact with them? Even more importantly, I began to wonder if I could learn how to be a better guy myself. Then (and this is the best part), I began to wonder if I could help others eliminate this wasted emotional energy. Could I show them how to tell the good guys from the bad guys in their work, social, and family lives and help them protect their inner circle of friends, coworkers, and family from the negative consequences of living, working, and otherwise dealing with untrustworthy people?

Sorting out those we *can* trust from those we *cannot* trust is the key. When we surround ourselves with trustworthy people, our problems are not necessarily eliminated, but problem solving certainly becomes much more manageable.

Thus began my journey to figure out how to tell the good guys from the bad guys. Along the way, I was hoping to learn how to be a better guy myself.

I interviewed and emailed questionnaires to hundreds of people. Some are CEOs of major multinational corporations, and some are employees on the manufacturing line. Some are pursuing careers and some are not. Some are retired. I simply asked people, "How do you tell the good guys from the bad guys in work and life?" I told them I wanted to know how they made decisions about whom they could and couldn't trust. I wanted to learn what strategies they used and I wanted to know when, how, and why they would ever give someone a second chance. I wanted to know how they work and/or live with people they know they can't trust. I never defined good or bad guys. I let everyone decide that on their own.

I hope you find the questions provocative, the insights enlightening, and the book a useful companion on your life's journey.

Chapter 1

What's Trust All About?

Do not trust all men, but trust men of worth; the former course is silly, the latter a mark of prudence.

—Democritus

TRUST IS IMPORTANT. When trust is present, professional and personal relationships thrive. However, like water, air, and electricity, it is something we often take for granted, and we don't realize its importance until it's gone! We can live without trust in our lives, but life isn't much fun.

Although everyone knows that trust is important and valuable to our relationships, nearly every one of us has felt the sharp sting of betrayal at one time or another. And, when trust is broken, relationships falter. But if trust is such an integral component of happy and successful lives, why do some people break it? And, knowing that someone could break your trust, we must ask the question: Whom *can* you trust?

COMING TO TERMS

Choosing someone to trust is not an easy decision. After all, trust is a willingness to be vulnerable—a willingness to take a risk that someone will not harm us. When we place our trust in the wrong person, the consequences can be severe. However, we initially allow ourselves to be vulnerable, because we have positive expectations of another's behavior.[1]

Not only is there an expectation that those we trust will not harm us, even when we are not present to monitor their behaviors, we also assume they will help us, even when we're not present to remind them.[2] The expectation is that the trusted party will work to protect—and even advocate for—our interests, or at least not conduct activities that will harm us in any way.

I'd like to think that my trusted confidants would actually advance my cause, even when I'm not in their presence. They'll mention me positively to others, defend my character if it is under attack, recommend me for potential jobs, or tell me the location of their favorite clothing store. In the vernacular, "They've got my back!"

Unfortunately, this is not always the case. That's why we should carefully consider whom we allow into our inner circle of trusted confidants.

TRUST IS MORE THAN MERE INSTINCT

The concept of trustworthiness and whom we should or should not let into our inner circle may seem obvious and simple, but it's not! Trust is complex. Many people claim that they have a strong instinct about whom they can and can't trust, almost a seat-of-the-pants belief they can sense who is and who isn't trustworthy. My research, however, has shown that what some people label as instinct is really just an accumulation of life experiences melded with reflective observation—in other words, experiential learning. Instinct in humans, unlike instinct in other species, is too strongly influenced by external factors—such as our upbringing, our inner circle of friends, family, neighbors, neighborhoods, and everything that touches our lives—to be considered pure.

What some people label as instinct or intuition could also easily become the basis for stereotyping. For example, some people's instincts might tell them not to get on an elevator with a leather-jacketed, tattooed person with spiked hair, or, if they do, to draw their personal belongings a bit closer. Some folks may have intuitions (that may later evolve into stereotypes) that women lack both the physical stamina and mental discipline necessary to lead our country. Others may falsely believe that most people can be trusted in work and life.

In its purest form, instinct has merit. For example, if we are hiking and we encounter a mountain lion, our instincts warn us to be fearful. However, our instincts can become flawed and influenced by the beliefs and behaviors of parents, neighbors, friends, teachers, and others.

Thus, while there are exceptions, instinct alone rarely works to predict trustworthiness. That kind of gut-level response is what comedian Stephen Colbert might call "trustiness." It might feel right, but watch out!

Our ability to gauge genuine trustworthiness is actually a learned behavior. It's based upon our past experiences. When we learn from those past experiences, we increase our success rate of identifying those people who are worthy of our trust. We can then begin to trust ourselves to make accurate judgments about trustworthiness in others. The Trust Rules Toolkit, developed for this book and explained in later chapters, discusses just how to do that.

SOME PSYCHOLOGICAL THEORY AS BACKGROUND

Ego psychologist Erik Erikson was perhaps the first to study the importance of trust to a successful and happy life. According to Erikson, most of us learn our lessons about trust and mistrust in early childhood. This was especially true for Erikson, who was abandoned by his father before birth. This event is believed to have led to his interest and work in identity and trust-related issues. As a child psychologist, Erikson refined previous thinking about the development of trust in human beings. And I have found a number of Erikson's observations reflected in those I interviewed for this book. For example, when asked whom they had most trusted in their lives, the most frequent answers interviewees gave were mothers, fathers, or grandparents.

Erikson believes that we not only need to learn to trust, but we also need to learn to mistrust, to avoid becoming gullible fools as adults. For Erikson, trusting too much (a maladaption) can be nearly as harmful as not trusting at all (a malignancy). The following story offers some insight into the downside of trusting too much.

It's Hard To Recover, Once We've Been Duped

Thomas couldn't believe it—he just couldn't believe it. Dave, the assistant manager at the community bank, had been pilfering money from cash deposits made by lifelong customers of the small community bank. No one had even suspected. Dave had "borrowed" money intended for individual depositors and put the money back, before the monthly statements were issued. Finally, Dave just didn't have enough money at the end of the month to return to the depositors' accounts. Ultimately, he was caught.

Thomas, the bank manager and Dave's boss, had granted Dave his unconditional trust. That Dave was untrustworthy never entered Thomas's mind. It wasn't until it was too late that he realized how wrong he had been to trust Dave so completely. Thomas had observed Dave had begun drinking a bit too much again, but he'd just brushed it off. The drinking had happened before, but Dave seemed to always be able to turn it around. Not this time, as Dave's overdrinking put him in a debt situation that caused his need to "borrow" the money from the bank where he worked.

As we might imagine, the incident wrecked Dave's career. What we might not imagine, however, is that the incident also wrecked Thomas's career—not because the company fired or demoted Thomas, but because Thomas could never recover from the fact he had misplaced his trust in Dave.

This story may sound familiar—just change the names, change the script. At some time in our lives, most of us will be duped by someone we thought we could trust. Our desire, of course, is to keep this from happening.

Finding the balance between trusting enough and trusting too much is important to becoming successful and well-adjusted adults. According to Erikson, if we resolve this *trust-mistrust* stage of development successfully, we have the wherewithal to manage and master the remaining developmental stages of our lives. Conversely, those of us who don't resolve this stage successfully, who develop malignancies or maladaptions, are likely to struggle throughout our lives with trust-related issues and become adults who may not be trustworthy ourselves.

THERE'S A LOT OF BETRAYAL GOING ON

We can easily see the impact of fractured trust in our own lives. Relationships are damaged when a trusted colleague, friend, spouse, partner, or family member betrays us, whether through lying, cheating, or otherwise not honoring and valuing the trusted relationship. The number of relationship betrayals associated with infidelity, now close to 25 percent for both men and women, speaks to the seriousness of this issue.[3] The following story is a poignant example of the far-reaching implications of betrayal in our personal lives.

Never Has Arrived

My wife of many years was someone I had thought I could always trust; she was my best friend. I knew this happened to other people who thought they had great marriages, but I never thought this would happen to me. I had been deceived for a long time; for nearly two years she was seeing someone else. I didn't even have an inkling this was happening. I learned I could be really gullible (despite the fact that I considered myself worldly and a huge success in business). Interestingly, while all the sex stuff was pretty hurtful, what was the most hurtful was finding out that she was a liar and so deceitful—that's the humiliating and degrading part of it all, and the part that's so hard to forget. I would have bet my life that she would NEVER do something like this. When I realized that someone I loved, and whom I know loved me, could lie and betray me so horribly, I began to think, what could someone do who didn't even care about me? I was very, very sorry to lose my wife, or at least, to lose the wife I thought I had. But over time, I became even sorrier that my relationship with trust and people in my work and life changed so dramatically. For me, it's taken the fun out of living.

—Nathan James, CEO, Multinational Manufacturing Company[4]

The feeling that we have no sense of who is and who isn't trustworthy is a difficult emotion to overcome, regardless of how successful the rest of our lives may appear to be. Does that mean we should hide from the possibility of being betrayed? Does it mean we should not live life to its fullest? No! It simply means we need to be more prudent with our trust-related decisions.

BETRAYAL IS FAR-REACHING

Other examples of the far-reaching implications of distrust in our lives can be found in the enormous scope of the betrayals by clergy in the Catholic Church, or by evangelicals caught in sexual predation. We're now all too aware that even those in our most trusted occupations have fallen short of our expectations regarding trust. We'll continue this discussion in a later chapter;

but for now, it's important to note that these supposedly *unconditional trust relationships* are sometimes the easiest to violate. Why? Because most of us don't want to doubt that those we trust the most would violate our trust in *any* way.

Trusted human relationships are the foundation of every organization, and these relationships allow people to work together to achieve remarkable results. What we observe at an individual level is also visible in the larger context of community, institutions, and organizations. It may be more difficult to observe because of the large number of people involved or the diversity of locations. The Josephson Institute of Ethics, a nonprofit, nonpartisan organization seeking to improve the ethical quality of our society, conducted a survey of 9,630 high school students. They found that young people are much more cynical than their elders and more likely to believe it is necessary to lie or cheat to get ahead in life. They also found that cheaters in high school are more likely as adults to lie to their spouses, customers, and employers. Previous studies showed that a disturbingly high number of students thought it was okay to lie or cheat to get ahead—60 percent had cheated on a test in the past year; 42 percent had lied or cheated to get ahead in some other way. Michael Josephson, the Institute's director, drew a disturbing conclusion from the data: *We have a hole in the moral ozone that is endangering society*.

And this deception does not stop once children graduate and enter the workforce. A recent book, *Trust Is Everything*, by Aneil and Karen Mishra reported that workplace trust is at an all-time low. These researchers claim that when trust is broken at the organizational level, there are negative implications for all stakeholders in the company, including employees, customers, clients, shareholders, and partners—all are affected, whether through reduced motivation, productivity, or performance. [5]

In companies where CEOs have broken trust, the results can be staggering; shareholders abandon the stock, employees give less effort or quit, and customers find other, more trustworthy alternatives. In some cases, the companies go out of business. The Enron example of the early 2000s continues to be the not-so-shining example of broken trust in organizations.

In an even broader sense, the media tell us that citizens no longer have high levels of trust in their political leaders. The result? Apathetic voters stay away from the polls, and those who *do* vote, toss out some incumbents, just for the sake of change.

It's not surprising that many people deem presidential elections to be campaigns for trust, as the voters are asked to determine:

- Whom do we trust to lead our country?
- Whom do we trust to make pivotal international relations decisions?
- Whom do we trust to keep our country fiscally responsible?
- Whom do we trust to maintain a country culture of trust and dignity on the domestic scene?

Once again, our charge—the charge of the voters—is to sort the good guys from the bad guys in public office and to determine whom we can and can't trust.

BETRAYAL IS BAD FOR EVERYONE

In organizations, the lower the level of trust, the higher the costs of managing employees. The economic impact can be measured by employee turnover, attitude surveys, length of time to hire, or similar metrics. This holds true throughout the organization. If employees trust their supervisor, the supervisor spends less time monitoring the employees' activities. If the organization trusts the CEO, a culture of trust permeates the entire organization. If there is trust in the company, then the tools of distrust, which include compliance tasks, many current human resources activities, and elaborate performance management systems—employee development processes and recruiting rules/guidelines—are no longer necessary.

Without organizational trust, the focus of every transaction revolves around issues of determining who has control and ensuring no one gets more than that to which they're entitled. In essence, time and energy are spent on policing, rather than developing, employees.

Likewise, in our personal lives, pursuing recreational activities takes less negative energy and is more enjoyable when we're in the company of trusted colleagues, friends, or family, rather than being saddled with those we don't trust. Personal relationships, based on full trust, make us more productive, effective, efficient, and focused in life and give us an anchor or touchstone, no matter what we do or where we go. These relationships give us the freedom to spread our wings.

IMAGINE THAT TRUST DOESN'T EXIST

Let's imagine some situations where trust doesn't exist and then consider the limitations this might place on our lives. Suppose that each time we leave town on a business trip, we worry that a business colleague will take credit for our work or even try to get our job. Imagine that a spouse/partner is unfaithful, or isn't adequately caring for our children, or isn't protecting our financial resources on the home front. In these instances, it would be difficult to concentrate on our objectives, nearly impossible to achieve our career-related goals, and even harder yet to maintain well-adjusted mental and physical health. We'd be frantic with anxiety. Ever feel that way?

Now let's look at a different situation in which trust is present. Successful business leaders are often quick to report that someone in their inner circle played an instrumental role in their successful lives and careers. During a recent conversation, John Morgridge, former CEO and Chairman Emeritus of Cisco Systems, sang the praises of his wife, Tashia Morgridge, freely giving her a share of credit for his success at Cisco Systems. He's the first to admit he could not have been so successful, had he not had a trusted confidant in his wife.

Similarly, Bill Davis, retired CEO and Chairman of the Board of Donnelly Corporation said to me, "In my personal life, I found Judy [his wife of many years], I never let her get away, and we meet many nice people because of her. That is my formula for finding trustworthy people in my personal life, and it has worked for years." For Davis, surrounding himself with *Good Guy* Judy Davis has helped him be a good guy himself and find even more good-guy associates.

Even the televised award shows showcase the trust factor, when teary-eyed actors (the sincere ones!) thank their parents for all the sacrifices they made to further their children's dreams. Consider professional athletes who take great pains to credit their coaches, mentors, or parents for pushing them to be their best and for never letting them settle for less. On the other hand, any time we hear someone brag about being a completely self-made success, don't we find ourselves asking how that could possibly be?

BUILDING ON ERIKSON

From Erikson's research and teaching, we learn that success in both business and life requires us to distinguish those we can trust from those we cannot. Erikson notes that we begin to learn this as children and continue to hone this skill throughout our lives. To be successful and enjoy life, we need to surround ourselves with people we can count on.

For business leaders, this skill is important because of the high stakes involved in leading large organizations. Great leaders *earn* the trust of their employees. We will have a more lengthy discussion of this in Chapter 12; but for now, remember that, for great leaders who have earned the trust of their employees, trust brings with it a companion—a willingness on the part of employees to maximize contributions and effort.

Similarly, building trusted family cultures is important in both our personal and family lives. The high stakes of the psyches of our children, spouses, partners, and friends demand it. As Erikson determined, childhood is a foundational time for learning how, when, and whom to trust. We'll discuss how to build more trusting family environments more fully in Chapter 11; but for now, let's remember that children who observe the broken trust bond of their parents are placed in a confusing situation. This situation may also impose a filter on those children's ability to successfully resolve important developmental stages. The family-trust bond remains important, even as children become adults—the influence of parents in trusting (and likewise untrusting) relationships can be passed from generation to generation.

PEER GROUPS: CHOOSE THEM WISELY, NO MATTER HOW OLD YOU ARE

We learn early on the importance of our peers to our development, whether for good or bad. Those of us who become socially healthy adults learn to resist peer pressure when friends are pushing us the wrong way and to accept it when it helps. If we surround ourselves with people who gossip, lie, or cheat, and are not careful with our trust, we become more and more accepting of these *bad-guy* behaviors. Fortunately, the opposite is also true. If we surround ourselves with people who have strong, positive values, their influence on us can be just as strong.

Our inner circle of friends reinforces certain behaviors and values, even when we're unaware this is happening. That's why it's critically important to select an inner circle that shares our true values. It's also essential to check that inner circle from time to time, to be sure those values are still in place. If we don't, the result can be disappointment in our lives at work and home, as we waste precious time and energy in relationships that sap our emotional resources. Alternatively, if we are reflective about our inner circle, we can make better decisions about what matters and focus our time on the positive aspects of work and life.

LOOKING AHEAD

We become even more grateful for our trusted relationships when we see enormous breaches of trust in the lives of others. Most of us want to be married or partnered with the 75 percent of people who are not betraying their spouses or partners. We also want to surround ourselves with trustworthy colleagues, clergy, CEOs, and politicians. How do we do that? And how do *we* become those people?

If we listen carefully as people talk about those they trust and how they decide to trust, we can identify signals to look for in those we think might be trustworthy. We see that those qualities can be useful in determining trust. The trust decision then becomes one we choose to make or not make, rather than arrive at by accident. It can be both exciting and empowering! Now, let's move on to the next chapter and get started!

NOTES

1.   Jennifer Dunn and Maurice Schweitzer, "Feeling and Believing: The Influence of Emotion on Trust," *Journal of Personality and Social Psychology* 88, no. 5 (2005): 736–48.

2.   Roger Mayer, James Davis, and David Schoorman, "An Integration Model of Organizational Trust," *Academy of Management Review,* 20 (1995): 709; Robert F. Hurley, "The Decision to Trust," *Harvard Business Review* (2006), September.

3.   John M. Grohol, "How Common is Cheating and Infidelity?" *World of Psychology*, March 2 (2013); Gary Stoller, "Infidelity Is in the Air for Road Warriors," USA-Today, April 19 (2007). Adrian J. Blow and Kelly Hartnett, "Infidelity in Committed Relationships II: A Substantive Review," *Journal of Marital and Family Therapy*, 31, no. 2 (2005): 217–233.

4.   The names of these people have been changed to protect anonymity.

5.   Aneil Mishra and Karen Mishra, *Becoming a Trustworthy Leader* (East Sussex: Routledge, 2013).

Chapter 2

Telling the Good Guys
from the Bad Guys at Work

It is easy to fool a man in the direction he wants to go.

—Maurice Schoenfeld, Founder, CNN

IN THE PREVIOUS CHAPTER we considered the fallibility of relying on intuition as a tool for determining trustworthiness. In the next few chapters we'll methodically analyze the consistent traits of *good guys*. But first, we need to know just what these traits are.

SOME METHODOLOGY

To discover the consistent traits of good guys, I interviewed and surveyed hundreds of people and then sorted the consistent responses into groupings. Analysis of this data led to the construction of a matrix. Then, extending this list of criteria, I created the Trust Rules Questionnaire (presented in Chapter 9). A tool that you, and I, can use to help determine whom we can trust to be part of our inner circle of life.

In this chapter we'll focus on twelve quotes from successful business leaders. Each quote contains one or more criteria these leaders have deemed characteristics of a trustworthy person in the workplace. After each of these interview snippets, we'll briefly discuss the trust-related insight. We'll extrapolate the core concepts from the interview snippets and add those measurable behaviors (characteristic from each insight) to the Trust Rules Questionnaire that we will use in Chapter 9.

Let's begin by thinking about whom we can trust in our workplaces and why.

TELLING THE GOOD GUYS
FROM THE BAD GUYS AT WORK

I spoke with CEOs of multinational corporations, leaders of smaller companies, and entrepreneurs. All were asked the open-ended question, "How do you tell the good guys from the bad guys in your work life? How do you decide whom you can and cannot trust?" I never defined *good guy*, yet everyone seemed to know just what I meant.

Why begin with business leaders? First, they are professional judges of people for their companies. They have spent their careers selecting, coaching, and rewarding or disciplining others, based at least partially on leadership behaviors that have their foundations in trust. Second, as part of their path to high-level positions, these leaders have had to think in-depth about their leadership style and how to gain the trust and respect of others. Third, their assessments of people have high stakes in terms of visibility—their shareholders, employees, and other constituents have a front-row seat when leadership decisions about people go well (replacing Steve Jobs with Tim Cook at Apple) or fail (Carly Fiorina at Hewlett-Packard). Because of these roles and judgments, business leaders should know a great deal about identifying good guys.

How do these leaders make the trust judgment? How do those with successful careers decide whom to let into their inner circle of confidants? The answer: They have developed, either on a conscious or subconscious level, an assessment process to guide their choices.

All those interviewed for this study were well aware of the importance of their inner circle of confidants to their business success. Some had clear, specific criteria by which they evaluated potential confidants, while others indicated they weren't consciously aware of their system for sorting good guys from bad guys. For them, this was an *ah ha* moment, as they first reflected on, and then articulated how they made this decision. Thinking about the question forced them to realize they *did* have an established protocol.

For economists, the term *opportunity cost* means the value of the best alternative forgone when a choice must be made between mutually exclusive alternatives under limited resources. Economists would say that the opportunity cost of not trusting is quite high—that the time we spend dealing with untrustworthy people could be used in much more productive endeavors.

Imagine, for example, that instead of having to spend time monitoring others' trustworthiness, business leaders could spend their time developing new organizational strategies, creating new products and services, and undertaking activities that enhance the company's bottom line.

Perhaps that's why the successful business leaders interviewed for this book have developed an expertise for figuring out whom they can and cannot trust. With extraordinary demands on their time and heavy pressures to succeed, they have little patience for nonproductive interactions. It is apparent that most have, consciously or subconsciously, used their lives as mini-research studies to figure out how to be better at weeding out the good guys from the bad guys in their work lives.

They learned from every interaction—some good, some bad—and attempted to not make the same "trustworthy" assessment mistake again.

That's what we want to do, learn from every interaction we have and not make the same mistakes in the future. Hopefully the lessons learned from these business leaders can help us all become better at sorting out the good guys from the bad guys in our work and personal lives.

So now, let's dip into the font of their collective wisdom!

Good Guys Played Well in the Sandbox

History repeats itself. So if you can get a feel for one's character over time, it should be a good predictor of their future behavior. If you can find out what was important to someone in their childhood, for the most part, it's a good predictor of their future actions. People who were good kids, with good values when they were teenagers and in college, and early in their career, are probably going to be the kind of people who have the values I like when they get older.

Robert A. Eckert, Chairman Emeritus, Mattel Inc.

Insights

Eckert relates the story of how he was hired at Kraft Foods, where he began his career. He explained that he'd interviewed all day long with Kraft executives. At the end of the day, he learned he had one more interview to go. This final interview was unscheduled, so he thought it might be important, with someone who rarely had time or hadn't wanted to commit until it was certain Eckert was a promising candidate. That final interview turned out to be with Keith Ridgway, the president of Kraft. Eckert still remembers being twenty-two years old, sitting on a red sofa on Peshtigo Court in Chicago (the former long-time corporate headquarters for Kraft Foods), answering questions about his childhood, family, and his values. Ridgway didn't want to know about Eckert's resume or his grades (other interviewers had made him jump through those hoops); Ridgway wanted to know what kind of *guy* Eckert was.

To this day, Eckert uses the same criteria. He wants to work with people who have good values. Eckert claimed that many people can learn the business, many people can learn to do the technical aspects of the job—what many people can't learn are good values. For both Eckert and Ridgway, developing and remaining loyal to solid values from childhood on is an important predictor of loyalty to colleagues and the company. These values don't have to come from a traditional family upbringing; they could have been taught and reinforced by childhood neighbors, mentors, parents, distant relatives, or even friends in the community.

———— •◆• ————

For Eckert, a characteristic of trustworthy people: ***Trustworthy people demonstrate good values throughout their history.***

Good Guys Live Their Values in Good Times and Bad

It's easy to be a great leader, spouse, parent, or friend when things are going smoothly. But it's how we distinguish ourselves when everything isn't going well that separates the good guys from the bad. And in the work world that's what we get paid for, doing well when things aren't going well. We have to deliver great results, while still living our values!

Richard H. Lenny, Former Chairman of the Board, President,
and CEO, Hershey Company

Insights

Trustworthy people work through problems, not around them. The untrustworthy flee when life gets tough. They may literally flee, by leaving the company or family space, or they might just flee emotionally and leave us to solve the problems on our own. The pressure might turn them into people we don't recognize: irate, irrational, and harmful.

In conversation with Lenny about good guys and bad guys in work and life, he related a story about a conversation he'd had with his ten-year-old daughter about bad guys. He began with the observation that he had decided long ago he would never let any one person drive him away; he would never run from a problem. He explained that his daughter was starting the fifth grade the day of our interview and was uncomfortable about school this year because *so-and-so* was in her class again—someone who had made her life a bit miserable. Lenny told his daughter that there are so-and-so's everywhere you work and live. You find them in the fifth grade and they just never go away. You have to learn how to live with them in ways that aren't destructive to you or them.

What sage advice to teach his daughter. Many of us would rather run from our problems than learn to deal with them, but running away solves nothing. As Lenny's advice to his daughter depicts, we have to confront our fears and our problems or we will never master them; they will master us. Whether in the workplace or in life, we have to live our values in good times and bad.

————— ◆ ——————

For Lenny, a characteristic of trustworthy people: *Good guys are good, even in difficult times.*

Good Guys Don't Keep Going Up the Down Escalator

Maintaining absolute integrity is one of the most important distinctions to be made when deciding whom we can and can't trust. Intelligence, admitting, and learning from mistakes are others—you just won't get far if you keep trying to go up the down escalator. One's self-awareness—the ability to recognize and understand one's own moods, emotions, and drives and their effect on others—is yet another important predictor.

James Kilts, former Chairman of the Board, President, and CEO, Gillette Co.

Insights

Kilts believes we have to first know ourselves before we can understand others. To paraphrase Aristotle, a life unexamined is a life of constant misunderstandings. Kilts also claims the baseline for allowing people into our inner circle of confidants should be unwavering integrity—daily demonstrations that behavior, not just words, match values.

It's interesting to consider how hard untrustworthy people *do* work—but at the wrong things! They work hard to convince us that they didn't do anything wrong, or that special circumstances influenced their behavior. They make excuses, rather than take responsibility.

Self-awareness is another important aspect for Kilts—people who are trustworthy understand how their moods and emotions may affect others in the workplace. Some examples we can all relate to:

- I didn't get enough sleep last night; I woke up grumpy.
- Maybe it was my fault Joe and I argued.
- There are things going on in my personal life that affect my moods today.
- I've got to be careful to not blame others for my mood.

———— • ◆ • ————

For Kilts, two characteristics of trustworthy people: *Trustworthy people admit and learn from their mistakes. They have a self-awareness of the ways their behaviors affect others.*

Good Guys Do Sweat the Small Stuff

I observe individual behavior very closely and frequently I look at what may appear to be "little things" to some, but to me are things that I believe indicate whether someone is a good guy or not. In a business setting, do individuals conduct themselves the same way when interfacing with someone from the housekeeping staff as they do with the CEO? Do they treat everyone the same, with the same amount of human dignity, regardless of their status? These things, in my view, provide insight into a person's character. What I am really saying is that there needs to be consistency in interacting with people at all levels. At the end of the day, honesty, integrity, trust, and treating people with respect is my ultimate benchmark of being a trustworthy person, either in a professional or in a personal setting. Sometimes it is the "small stuff" that makes the difference.

Robert L. Parkinson, Jr., Chairman and CEO,
Baxter International Inc.

Insights

We've all seen the busy executive who treats the security guard or receptionist as some kind of lesser being. Or the so-called friend who takes you to dinner and then abuses the waiter. Are they showing off their position or status—or are they simply rude? Does it matter? Why would we not expect people to treat others with respect and dignity under all circumstances?

Parkinson offers an insight that many of us have had to learn the hard way—by experience. If we continue to trust someone who is selectively kind or honest (even though we may be one of the lucky ones right now), we should not be surprised when someday they turn on us.

———•◆•———

For Parkinson, characteristics of trustworthy people: *Trustworthy people treat all people the same, regardless of level in the hierarchy (work or social), and they demonstrate consistent good behaviors.*

You Can't Judge a Good Guy by the Cover

People who are smarter, prettier, and/or well spoken often appear to be trustworthy. But being a trustworthy person has nothing to do with these things. Instead, it's all about the person's intentions and concern for others. So how do I tell? I try to understand people's motivations: Do they only do and say things for their own benefit (directly or indirectly), or are they helping others just because they can?

Trustworthy people are happy to have "free riders"—people who benefit from their actions at no extra cost to either party involved. Those who are untrustworthy will only interact with you when there is something in it for them.

Ariel Poler, Founder/Investor, I/PRO, Topica, Kana Software, and LinkExchange

Insights

People in positions of power have the opportunity to take advantage of those who have less power. It's easy to do but good guys just don't do it.

A key aspect of Poler's insight is to have an understanding of whether someone's intentions and motivations are self-serving, or does this person willingly help others without any expectation of a return? This aspect has to do with the concept of *paying it forward;* giving unselfishly—those *random acts of kindness.*

Poler knows it's not about what people look like, how well they are educated, or how much money they have; it's about people's intentions and concern for others.

———•◆•———

For Poler, a characteristic of trustworthy people: *Trustworthy people have positive qualities other than just good looks, a good education, and wealth; they have good intentions and a sincere concern for others.*

Good Guys Separate Fact from Fiction

Rarely does anyone know the whole story about an event or business decision. But it's easy to want to gain attention or status by having the facts, or pretending to have them. We all use our personal assumptions and experience to fill in the blanks of a situation. We need to understand the difference between adding information that helps make sense of the puzzle and providing inaccurate information— something we claim to know because it makes us feel or look good—that makes the situation worse. Trustworthy people tell listeners whether they are sharing facts or their own assumptions and admit when they know nothing at all.

Elaine Patterson, Unocal, GM,
People Development

Insights

Trustworthy people value being perceived as open and honest in the moment much more than being seen as smart right now but proven wrong later. Someone who has all the answers either needs to impress everyone or control everyone. I'm reminded of the humorous quote by Mark Twain: "I am not one of those who, in expressing opinions, confine themselves to the facts." Twain gets to the heart of Patterson's issue: When someone is more concerned about knowing it all, rather than making a contribution, that person is short-changing the decision-making process and the team and the organization suffer. Patterson notes we can't possibly have selected the best course of action, if we consider only our own (sometimes flawed) information.

————•◆•————

For Patterson, a characteristic of trustworthy people: *Trustworthy people admit when they don't know something and welcome helpful criticism.*

Good Guys Are Honest Without Violating Trust

The biggest single factor people respect in a "good guy" is honesty.

However, everyone at work has to be dishonest sometimes by acts of omission (e.g., you don't tell the rank and file you are considering a major downsizing until you are ready, you don't tell someone they may be fired by the CEO if you have been asked not to). A good guy tries to be honest at all times and finds a way to communicate the things he cannot be honest about, without violating a trust.

Daniel McCarty, retired CEO, American Crystal Sugar Company

Insights

Trust and truth are intimately connected. We spend time teaching children to tell the truth. As we grow older, we find out that absolute truths are sometimes hard to find, as there are multiple perspectives on any situation. In business, there isn't always a single truth, so mature people learn to express their opinions in a nonjudgmental way and encourage others to do the same. They speak honestly and openly but recognize there are valid opinions elsewhere. Good guys find thoughtful and diplomatic ways to give others a different view of the truth. In doing this, they teach us something about seeing an event or person from all sides. It would be much easier to simply agree with what the other person believes or says. We could say that it is also less risky to a relationship, but it doesn't make for a very deep and trusting one. The point is, even in difficult emotional situations, telling the truth is always the best formula and doing so gives those hearing our words the respect they deserve. It demonstrates that we are consistently respectful to others in difficult times and will be the same with them.

————— •◆• —————

For McCarthy, a characteristic of trustworthy people: *Trustworthy people demonstrate absolute integrity and know that everyone deserves the respect of the truth; they are able to take another's perspective and are aware of multiple "truthful" perspectives.*

Good Guys Help Keep Me Good

The people I let into my inner circle help keep me sharp... those in my inner circle of confidants will fearlessly give me feedback... they will relentlessly keep me on track with my life at work and beyond. They pro- vide unconditional help and have an unconditional interest in my well-being. I try to be the same kind of friend to them.

Douglas Conant, *New York Times* Best Selling Author, Chairman Kellogg Executive Leadership Institute and former CEO, Campbell Foods.

Insights

People often value their inner circle because they are on the same page or see life the same way. Conant reminds us that people who mindlessly agree with us and don't challenge our thinking may not make the best confidants. His inner circle adds value to his life by providing unconditional help—they give him the gift of their insights, unconditionally. He doesn't have to call them; they are alert in a manageable, thoughtful way that enhances his ability to be an effective human being. He trusts their thinking, trusts their instincts, and trusts their intentions. Those he lets into his inner circle help him be a better person.

———— •◆• ————

For Conant, a characteristic of trustworthy people: *Trustworthy people voluntarily, in constructive ways, tell us when we're doing something wrong.*

You'd Introduce Good Guys to Your Mother

I've learned that the good guys are those I'd take home to meet my family. When I'm trying to assess someone's overall level of "good," I ask myself, would I expose this person to my family? Is this someone I'd intro- duce to my kids, wife/ spouse/partner, parents? If I can't, or am unwilling to introduce someone to my family, there must be some "bad" reason why.

B. Gregory Stroh, former CEO, Custom Industries

Insights

For many cultures and societies, *mother* is the symbol of the ultimate confidant, the person who approves of us unconditionally and the one person we can trust, no matter what. While *your* mother may not be your most trusted confidant, the symbol in Stroh's insight is important. If there's someone in your work or personal life you would not or cannot introduce to your spouse, children, family, friends, or other trusted confidants, examine why you feel that way. There's probably some untrustworthy reason why.

———•◆•———

For Stroh, a characteristic of trustworthy people: *Trustworthy people can be introduced to your family and other confidants, without qualifiers.*

"No" Shakes Out a Lot of Bad Guys Quickly

Bad guys/con artists/shallows/disloyals are capable of being very charming and persuasive—as long as they are getting their way. So I set up a situation to say NO and monitor the reaction. The word NO shakes out a lot of people quickly.

Tom Baker, President, John T. Baker
& Associates, Executive Search

Insights

Good guys understand that people in their inner circle may have to say *no* to one of their requests or will sometimes have differing opinions on important issues and decisions. Good guys make every effort to see the other side and assess the situation objectively and not based simply on whether they win or lose.

I'm reminded of the great football coach and legend, Vince Lombardi, often quoted as saying, *"Show me a good loser, and I'll show you a loser."* While this philosophy may work well in the sports world, it doesn't work well in personal situations, where sometimes we have to lose an argument or a decision. Good guys are skilled at doing this in ways that allow everyone involved to maintain dignity and respect. They neither take everything personally nor view each interaction as a referendum on their personality or intellect.

Tough times, handled well, can bond us more closely to colleagues, friends, and family and increase the level of trust we have in each other. Tough times, handled poorly, split us apart. Baker reminds us that the good guys are those that surface when the answer is *No*.

————•◆•————

For Baker, a characteristic of trustworthy people: ***Trustworthy people respond in healthy ways, even when they don't get their way.***

Good Guys Know It's All about Playing Fair

Bad guys are good guys who've grown above the law or social norm in their own minds. The belief that the "law" or "rule" doesn't include me is what moves good guys to the bad guy bucket. The bad guys think they de- serve some unfair benefit in work or life more than others.

Good guys genuinely consider others in their lives and believe in the people around them who depend on them. Bad guys don't care and usually end up hurting others.

Richard E. Bailey, COO, Landauer Corporation

Insights

We all know people who live their lives as if *It's all about me*. Every action, decision, or movement they make stems from how they'll be affected. Bailey claims such people, in every instance, place their needs, emotions, and desires above others. Do you know someone who doesn't like to follow the rules—ever? Or someone who thinks he deserves more than others just because of who he is or what he has achieved? Do you know someone who is overly aggressive, doesn't play fair in negotiations, conflict situations, or in life in general? Someone who has one set of rules/norms for himself and another set for everyone else?

Immanuel Kant claimed some behaviors are categorically wrong. They are wrong at any time, place, and in any society.[1] For Kant, removing yourself from the rules and treating yourself as an exception to universal truths is always wrong, regardless of context. Like Kant, Bailey claims that when we think that laws or rules do not include us, or we deserve some unfair benefit, we've moved into the bad-guy bucket.

————•◆•————

For Bailey, characteristics of trustworthy people: *Trustworthy people hold themselves to the same standards they establish for others and they genuinely consider others in their lives.*

Good Guys Don't Do Bad Things, Just Because They Can

When I'm deciding whom to put in the good-guy bucket, whom to let into my inner circle of confidants, I look for behaviors that demonstrate a moral current— that "intangible" quality that prompts you to recognize they will always try to do the right thing. It's not just that they will do the smart thing, but that they will do the "right thing." I try to find these moral dilemmas and I observe how my inner circle conducts themselves and how they weigh in on these moral dilemmas. Are they willing to do something just because they can, or because it's legally right to do so; or, do they want to do the right thing? It's like trying to reach inside the soul of a person, because at the end of the day, that's what's going to drive that person as they make their tough decisions when I'm not around.

Norm Blake, former Chairman, President and CEO,
USF&G Corporation

Insights

Blake recounted a time when he fired someone who could "knock the ball out of the park," yet was disrespectful to those with whom he worked. Blake knew the disrespect would eventually lead to long-term demise of the organizational culture.

Blake considers the issue even broader than one of disrespect. He expected the leaders in his organization to model the company's core values and preserve the personal dignity of every individual. He put this individual on a *get-well program*, in essence, a probationary period during which the person had the opportunity to commit to a remedial action plan and correct his leadership and management style. After a six-month period with little improvement, Blake asked for the person's resignation. The health of his organization and the welfare of his workforce demanded it.

———— • ◆ • ————

For Blake a characteristic of trustworthy people: ***Trustworthy people do the right thing.***

SUMMARY

In this chapter we've seen what successful business leaders had to say about whom they could and could not trust in their workplaces. The insights they have gained along the way to the top of their professions are useful to all of us. Thus, taken collectively, their recommendations provide the basis for building the Trust Rules Questionnaire that encompasses the characteristics extracted from each quote. This Trust Rules Questionnaire, to be presented in Chapter 9, can then be used to help us better predict who is and isn't trustworthy. But first, in the next chapter, let's examine the characteristics of trustworthy people in our *personal lives*.

NOTE

1.   Immanuel Kant, *Foundations of the Metaphysics of Morals*, trans. Lewis White Beck (Indianapolis: Bobbs-Merril, 1976).

Chapter 3

Telling the Good Guys
from the Bad Guys in Life

If you can't be a good example, then you'll just have to serve as a horrible warning.

—Anonymous

MOST GOOD GUYS HAVE A CREDO that guides their behavior—a set of principles that provides a moral compass to their actions and enables them to behave and interact in ways that allow themselves and others to maintain safe, peaceful, and trusting relationships. Good guys make the active decision to live their lives as good people—it doesn't just happen. For us, the task is to figure out who *are* those good guys—those people with whom we will be safe. After all, trusting others is all about learning with whom we are safe and knowing who is looking out for our welfare as much as they are looking out for their own, whether in the workplace or in our personal lives.

The preceding chapter provided insights about telling good guys from bad guys at work. Some of the quotes in this chapter also come from successful business leaders, but this time the focus is on our personal lives. The questions were, "How do you tell the good guys from the bad guys in your personal life? How do you know whom you can and can't trust in life?"

Again, at the end of each quote, I've captured a characteristic of a good guy (a trustworthy person) that is an actual measure of a person's trustworthiness in the personal sector. We'll meet these characteristics again in the Trust Rules Questionnaire, depicted in Chapter 9, along with those we've already listed from Chapter 2. Some of the characteristics we discovered in the previous chapter on assessing trust in the workplace show up here as well, along with new ones. Hopefully, the slightly different take will be useful to you, or the similarities will make you think twice. Later on, we will discuss these similarities, and especially differences, to better understand the implications for our own lives.

Bad Guys Cheat at Golf and at Work

People tend to retain a good or bad character in all areas of life. For example, if someone cheats on the golf course, I'd assume that he or she will cheat in other areas of life as well. If a person was underhanded in business, I'd assume that his or her personal relationships were also filled with hypocrisy. Those who cheat at little things will probably cheat at the big things also. Good guys don't have shades of the truth.

Joseph D. McGuire, New York State
Supreme Court Justice

Insights

Being a New York State Supreme Court Justice gives one an opportunity to see lots of good and bad guys and to develop criteria to know the differences between them. Justice McGuire claims bad guys are always looking for an edge; they are willing to skirt the truth to get what they want. Good guys are honest, unpretentious, and looking to do right in both their work and personal lives. We hear people talk about separating their work lives from their personal lives, as if it were the norm. But is that reality or wishful thinking? It may take some time for one part of life to catch up with the other, but I'll bet we can all think of people who saw one part of their lives crumble, then the other. That's not accidental—it's inevitable. Good guys count all their shots! Good guys don't pick and choose when and if they will be a good guy; it's consistency of their behaviors that's the best measure.

————— • ◆ • —————

For Justice McGuire, a characteristic of trustworthy people is: **Trustworthy people don't have shades of truth; they have consistent good behaviors.**

Good Guys Don't Try To Cover Up Mistakes

It is gratifying when our society accepts that we are flawed human beings. And, that as a society, we respect people who acknowledge when they have done something wrong, reflect on that bad behavior, and understand what they did and why they did it. We are less forgiving of the dishonesty that surrounds a cover-up.

Randy Cohen, *New York Times*
Magazine Columnist

Insights

Cohen points out that it is cowardly to engage in a cover-up when we've made a mistake. When a friend, sibling, spouse/partner does something wrong, admits it, and is ready to pay the consequences, this person is considered trustworthy. In most instances, those consequences are that we trust them even more, because of their ability to be honest in a difficult situation.

If we want to be good guys, it's critically important to continually work to understand why we behave the way we do. Understanding the *why* part of our behavior is what may prevent us from continually making the same mistakes.

————•◆•————

For Cohen, a characteristic of trustworthy people: ***Trustworthy people admit when they've done something wrong, and learn from it.***

Good Guys Can Put Themselves in My Shoes

To me, good guys can put themselves in others' shoes, or can see themselves in situations others may be in and are then able to understand why others react or act in the way they do. Bad guys, on the other hand, see only one side of an issue; only how the situation affects them. They think their opinion is right; their action or reaction is the only correct one. In a word, compassion is what separates good guys from bad guys.

Gary Brown, Tire Builder, Goodyear Tire
and Rubber Company

Insights

Good guys are able to empathize with others' situations and can take another's perspective. They can assess how they might react if they were forced to live another life. They are able to understand that as our point of view changes, our reactions/behaviors may be different as well. In essence, Brown is saying that in our personal lives, the good guy is able to identify with and have compassion for those less fortunate (less fortunate cognitively, emotionally, economically, and/or socially).

——— • ◆ • ———

For Brown, a characteristic of trustworthy people: *Trustworthy people have compassion and empathy for others. They can see another's point of view/take another's perspective.*

Good Guys Don't Tell Themselves Lies

When I'm judging whether people are good guys and whether I can trust them, I look to see how well they "know" themselves. Good guys are truthful to themselves and others; they have a sense of integrity about the people that they are; they don't pretend to be something they aren't. For me, people who are honest with themselves are more likely to be honest with me.

Mary Honecker, wife, mother,
grandmother, caregiver

Insights

As Honecker observes, the most dangerous guys of all in our personal lives are those who don't really know themselves or who present themselves as something or somebody they are not. In doing so, they demonstrate they don't like who they really are, so they must pretend they are something else. They might appear charismatic and nice, yet be selfish and untrustworthy.

These people can fool us for a very long time and can fool themselves even longer. What's the problem with those who don't trust themselves enough to tell themselves the truth? They are never able to learn from their mistakes.

———•◆•———

For Honecker, a characteristic of trustworthy people: ***Trustworthy people demonstrate absolute authenticity with themselves and others; they have a healthy self-awareness.***

Bad Guys Aren't As Smart As They Think They Are

When it comes to words, I take special care at the onset of a new professional or personal relationship to listen carefully for contradictions in data, facts, etc., that are shared. Most people are not as smart as they think they are—they'll contradict themselves, if they aren't telling the truth. I also assess whether promises, deadlines, follow-ups, etc., are consistently kept and/or met. If someone is sincere and trustworthy, they'll follow through on promises—to return a phone call, to keep a date—deadlines, etc., without excuses or, in the worst case, total disregard.

Kimberly Evans, Marketing Operations Director,
Under Armour

Insights

Evans advises us to be on guard for contradictions between what people say and what they do. Evans also conveyed to me that it's a good idea to learn what others think about how trustworthy someone is. It's not uncommon to check out a new person with people we already know and trust. We all have personal reference-check mechanisms. Having trusted friends vouch for someone provides comfort, as well as a way of quickly deepening a new relationship. When we have a reference, it's easier to move quickly through the observations of whether the new person will keep to deadlines, follow through with promises, or offer assistance without our asking. Yet, according to Evans, we should still look for tangible cues—behaviors and actions, not words—when deciding whom we can and can't trust.

———— •◆• ————

For Evans, a main characteristic of trustworthy people in our personal lives: *Trustworthy people's behavior matches their "talk."*

Good Guys Can Set Aside Their Own Needs

When someone can set aside his or her own needs and feelings and take into account the other person's needs and interests when making decisions, that person is trustworthy in my eyes.

Anna Lieblich, PhD, MSW, Clinical Faculty,
The Family Institute at Northwestern University

Insights

There is a vulnerability associated with fully trusting other people in our personal lives. When we trust others, we expect that we are safe with them and that they will care for our feelings and not harm us. We further expect that they are aware that emotional harm, lying, cheating, and condescension can be just as harmful to us as physical harm.

One of my interviewees recalled a college friend, much wealthier than the rest of her friends. This friend did go to Bermuda for spring break but also took great pains to blend in with the rest of her friends. She never suggested splurges at restaurants they couldn't afford and never used her money in condescending ways. This behavior contrasted with one roommate's boyfriend, who did that all the time. He would want to go to expensive places, then offer to pay, as if he were doing everyone a favor. While the offer to pay was presented as a kindness, it was clearly done to impress the rest. The arrogant payer was the only one who didn't know the difference.

———— •◆• ————

For Lieblich, a characteristic of trustworthy people: *Trustworthy people demonstrate they know how their own behaviors affect others; they look out for others even when their own interests are at stake.*

Good Guys Won't Let Me Be Bad

I trust someone, after a time, because they have never lied to me, cheated me, condescended to me, betrayed me, or humiliated me. They have supported me, but also have not hesitated to tell me if they think I'm behaving badly or doing something that isn't in my best interest or that of someone else. They won't be a partner to my bad judgments. They won't let me be bad.

Patricia Schaeffer, Founding Partner,
Talent Strategy Partners, LLC

Insights

Schaeffer maintains how important it is to have friends who aren't cowardly in their friendships. They care enough about us to readily let us know when we are doing something wrong.

A wise professor of mine from Northwestern University, Dr. Tom Cook, used to say, *"Our enemies can be our best friends."* His reasoning was that our enemies will tell us what we are doing wrong, and our friends are often too cowardly to do so. Contrastingly, Schaeffer argues that the best of all worlds is to have trusted friends who *are* willing to tell us when we are misbehaving, even when it might be emotionally difficult to do so. We can only wonder if some rift in the family, with friends, or in the workplace could have been prevented if someone had said, "You're behaving so badly and being hurtful to innocent people. If you don't change your behavior, I'll no longer be your friend."

————•◆•————

For Schaeffer, a characteristic of trustworthy people: *Trustworthy people help us be better people; they won't let us be bad.*

You Can Tell the Good Guys in the Last Inning of the Game

I hate to use sports analogies; however, I do believe there is some relevance. When the game is sailing along and all the breaks are going your way, average players look pretty good. However, in difficult situations, the fourth quarter, the last inning of a tie game, the big-time players rise to the top. They want to lead the way. Sometimes that means they take the ball and run. Other times, they hand it off to others. The key point is they find ways to win or at least give it one heck of a try. I believe the same is true in life, outside of work. The good guys are there to help no matter what the circumstance. They don't run away from problems, they work through them with you, and are not friends only when it is convenient or easy to do so.

Ray DeRiggi, President Dole Foods

Insights

Good guys are those you want in the foxhole with you. You want them around when life gets tough, because you know they'll be there when you need them. They understand life isn't always perfect and they work with you to solve difficult work and life problems. It's during these tough times that the authentic good guys surface and rise above the crowd by never letting us down.

The OK guys out there sometimes seem like really good guys, until they are placed in a difficult situation. Then, when the going gets tough, these OK guys sometimes turn into the bad guys and do what suits them best, without assessing how their actions affect others. It's the authentic good guys that want to be part of the solution, not the problem, whether it means they get to be the star in the show or just a walk-on. They want the team, at home or in the workplace, to succeed, and they get pleasure or recognition from a combined effort, not just from their own contribution.

———•◆•———

For DeRiggi, a characteristic of a trustworthy person: *Good guys are there for us in good times and bad.*

Good Guys Have the Same Story Whether You're with Them or Not

Aside from the obvious bad behaviors, such as lying, cheating, stealing, stepping on others to get ahead, and discrimination, I use a simple rule of consistent behavior to spot a good guy in my world. I think you watch how a person treats other people and how they talk to them face-to-face and how they talk about them when they are not present. If these behaviors are consistently kind, just, respectful, and dignified, then you have found a good guy.

Fran Daly, PhD, Director, Costin Institute,
Midwestern University

Insights

We've probably all seen people who can rant and rave about another person's faults, then the next day see them laughing it up with the person they were just berating the day before. Or we've all been around the doting husband/wife/partner that's doting when that partner is around and doting on someone else when that partner isn't. Good guys don't do that, and if we decide to trust people who do, we are in for some surprises. People who are trustworthy have consistent behaviors, whether you are with them or not.

————•◆•————

For Daly, a characteristic of trustworthy people: *Trustworthy people speak the same of people, whether in their presence or not.*

Good Guys Have Stories That Stick Together

I enjoy people whose "story" sticks together, in that their lifestyle and friendship seem interwoven. The people that offer to help me and then follow through are the same ones that are generous with their time as a volunteer or a "giver" in some other fashion. They may have a concern and act to help in the global sense. There is congruence between what they talk about and how they behave.

Braggarts are a total turn-off to me. Generally, I feel the bragging is total compensation for what the person doesn't have. The bad guys to me have all the wrong motives for friendship. Their life objectives aren't in sync with mine. Interactions with them reduce the quality of your life. During interactions with these people, you waste valuable time and energy trying not to show your disinterest (on the best days) and disdain (on the worst judgmental days).

Louisa Levy, Nutritionist-Nurse Educator,
Lake Forest Health & Fitness Institute

Insights

In many cases, these good guys tell us about the rest of their lives in matter-of-fact, down-to-earth ways, giving us examples as explanations, but not seeking any special attention or reward. They're not trying to impress us with these stories, just revealing more of themselves. They put their money or time where their mouths are. They are also consistent in their talk and behaviors. We don't see good guys talking as if they are strong family people, and then later engaging in activities that are selfish and harmful to their families. They live their values in everything they do.

———•◆•———

For Levy, a characteristic of trustworthy people is: *Trustworthy people genuinely consider others in their lives; they are willing to share their time, space, money, and friends.*

You Can Tell Good Guys by Ways They Treat Their Spouses/Partners and Others

I closely observe people's behavior when assessing the nature/extent of their goodness. How does an individual treat/talk about/interact with his spouse/partner, administrative support, guy at the hotel check-in, or waitress at the restaurant. Not just when they are around, but when they aren't there, also. I think that I learn the most when the individual does not know they are being monitored.

For personal relationships, I focus much more on the spouse/partner. How people treat those who are supposedly the most important people in their lives is an important predictor of whether I can trust them or not. How will they treat me, if they are treating their dearest that way?

Paul Kasper, Principal, American
Securities Capital Partners

Insights

It makes sense. The ways we treat our family, those with whom we have multiple goals aligned (e.g., children, a checkbook, extended family), are great predictors of how we will treat others. Wasn't it former presidential candidate, Ross Perot, who said, "If your wife and children can't trust you, why should I?"

———•◆•———

For Kasper, characteristics of trustworthy people: *Trustworthy people treat everyone the same regardless of hierarchy, and, especially their loved ones whether they are around to observe him or not.*

Beware of Those in Distress—Sometimes They Turn Into Bad Guys

If people are under severe distress, broke, facing serious consequences, etc., then they will do things I would never expect. I think most people can be trusted to a degree, until they are under pressure or are in a situation that could have serious consequences for them. If that occurs, it is difficult to tell if a person will "crack" or hold the line. I've been burned by people in those situations before. I never allow myself to forget that people can sometimes change when they are placed in situations that challenge them beyond their mental and emotional capabilities.

Eric Hornbeck, Production Manager,
Pinnacle Foods Corporation

Insights

Sometimes life challenges us in ways beyond our ability to cope. Hornbeck isn't suggesting we mistreat these people; quite the contrary, he is merely suggesting we should be wary of placing trust in them during these difficult times.

Think about times we've heard about a poor decision someone made during desperate times. Invariably, their close friends responded by saying, "*If you had told us that, we would have helped or done something different, or intervened.*" This is the sort of guy Hornbeck is, one we would call when we need help or support. He reminds us that desperate people can make bad decisions, and we need to be careful about granting them unconditional trust in those circumstances. It's really, *really* good guys who can be good even when things go *really* wrong.

———•◆•———

For Hornbeck, a characteristic of trustworthy people: *Trustworthy people respond in healthy ways, even when things go wrong; but, if someone is in a crisis, be sure to know they may not be as trustworthy as they once were.*

SUMMARY

We've gathered more advice and tips from this chapter about how to tell the good guys from the bad guys. Combined with the tips in Chapter 2, these insights can provide important information about the characteristics of a trustworthy person. Each of the insights from Chapters 2 and 3 (summarized below) will now become part of the Trust Rules Questionnaire.

Good guy characteristics:

- A history that demonstrates good values.
- Likely to respond in a healthy way, when things go wrong.
- Admits and learns from mistakes.
- A self-awareness that demonstrates knowledge of how his or her behavior affects others.
- Treats everyone the same, regardless of level in the hierarchy (work or social).
- Demonstrates consistent good behaviors.
- Have positive qualities, other than just good looks, a good education, and wealth.
- Never takes advantage of others with his/her own good looks, education, or wealth.
- Admits when he/she doesn't know something.
- Demonstrates absolute integrity.
- Genuinely considers others.
- Voluntarily, in useful ways, tells me when I do something wrong.
- Helps me be a better person.
- I would introduce this person to my family and other trusted confidants.
- Respond in a healthy way, when they don't get their way.
- Hold themselves to the same standards they establish for others.
- Does the right thing.
- This person sticks by others in bad/tough times.
- This person speaks the same of people, whether in their presence or not.
- This person is likely to share resources (time, space, money, friends).

In the next chapter we'll continue to explore these important characteristics and examine similarities and differences in how to apply them in different work and life settings. Be sure to refer back often to the more complete explanations of each of these characteristics as depicted in Chapters 2 and 3.

Chapter 4

Comparing Work and Life Trust Rules

The unknown could be justified with even the most rudimentary form of logic, for someone who wanted to believe.

—Brad Stroh, *The Dharma King*

THE QUOTES IN CHAPTERS 2 and 3 are representative of those gathered during the interviews and email surveys I conducted for this book. The characteristics of trustworthy people extracted from each quote are the basis for the Trust Rules Questionnaire. We'll discuss the Trust Rules Questionnaire later in the book (Chapter 9), but for now, let's take a look at how the tips to sort the good guys from the bad guys at work differ from those for sorting good guys from bad guys in our personal lives.

COMPARING WORK AND LIFE INSIGHTS

As can be seen from the previous two chapters, there is a significant amount of overlap between the work and life trust rules. These similarities demonstrate that there are some core characteristics of the good guy that hold true in any situation at any time. It is interesting to note, however, that there were some key differences and omissions noted between our work and personal lives. We will be exploring these differences within this chapter. But first, let's begin this comparison with the work rules we should consider in our personal lives.

PLAY IT AGAIN, SAM

When assessing a potential personal confidant in our personal lives, few mentioned the importance of examining a person's history or past behaviors in predicting future behaviors. Why do we seem to worry less about personal history, when we are assessing friends outside of work? We may think we know family and friends better than business associates, but do we? If so, then why do we continue to be shocked and dismayed at some breaches of trust in our personal lives, suggesting we may not know friends and family as well as we think we do? One theory for why this occurs is that there is much more emotion wrapped up in our personal life trust decisions than in our work trust decisions, and that emotion can make the trust decision a bit messier. Our emotions can influence us to ignore or deny these characteristics in others with whom we have a personal and emotional relationship. Remember the famous quote, "Love is blind." This holds true for trust as well. Emotions can play a large role in our decisions of whom we can and cannot trust, and sometimes not in a beneficial way. For example, in our personal lives where emotions have a greater influence than in our work lives, we may, incorrectly, be more willing to think that someone who mistreats others may treat *us* better or differently. This is a dangerous assumption and one that could cause of a lot of disappointment and negative emotions later on. In the workplace, however, we would rarely make this mistake.

In the workplace few of us would want to be on a team with someone we knew had failed miserably on a previous task or relationship, or whom we knew had lied, cheated, or been disloyal in other work endeavors. In our workplaces, we are much more careful about considering people's past history of behavior. We just wouldn't take that risk and are more certain they would treat us similarly to how we had seen them behave/perform in the past and with others. We seem more cerebral about these decisions in our work setting—our emotions play less of a role in our decisions about relationships. But why is this? Well, in the workplace, the cost/benefits are more immediate and sometimes tangible, perhaps because our careers and paychecks are on the line. In fact, a recent article in *Business Insider* specifically addressed the differences between work friends and what they referred to as *real* friends, those in your personal life. They argued "the difference between your work friends and your real friends is that people you work with have the potential to directly influence or affect your career in a big way."[1]

In our personal lives, we operate quite differently. A person will marry someone who cheated on a previous spouse, or who fled to another state to avoid paying child support, or who lied about a criminal record, or who just can't hold a job. We seem more willing to ignore the disturbing facts in our personal lives than in our work lives and are more likely to create the illusion of a trustworthy person that simply doesn't exist. Yet, examining another person's history is a vital part of the trust assessment process in both our personal and our work lives.

The next important step is analyzing these past behaviors to make important predictions about future behaviors. Someone who has been untrustworthy in the past, or who is currently untrustworthy with others, especially when we've observed this firsthand, is likely to be untrustworthy with us as well.

DO LOOKS OR APPEARANCE AFFECT OUR TRUST DECISIONS?

It seems we are more easily fooled in our personal lives by physical appearance, education, or wealth, than we are in the workplace. Perhaps it is fun in the short term to align ourselves with folks who are smarter, prettier, wealthier, or better educated. They may provide us with entrance to special social events or invitations to spend time with the *in crowd* or be able to take us places we would never be able to go on our own merit. So, we pretend they are good guys, when they really are not!

But in the workplace, where a project must be completed or our careers are at stake, if Mr. or Ms. Good-looking, Wealthy, or Well-Educated isn't reliable and trustworthy, we don't want any of them on our team. We simply don't care about their pedigrees, looks, or personal wealth. We don't care where they can take us. We care about their actions and behaviors—their performance. The lesson here is that we should be just as results-focused in our personal lives.

You've heard the line, "All that glitters is not gold." But those aren't the correct words. The words are from Shakespeare's play *The Merchant of Venice* and the line reads, "All that Glisters is not gold." *The Merchant of Venice* is a play in which money and appearances significantly influenced behavior and few things are as they appear. As this analogy suggests, sometimes trusting what we hear, without putting the words to the test, can corrupt our thinking and behaviors about trust-related issues.

LOOK WHO'S COMING TO DINNER

An important strategy from Chapter 2, where we assessed trusted behaviors in our work confidants, concerns our willingness to introduce someone from our work life to our family, friends, and other trusted confidants. Think about it! We rarely say to our personal confidants, "I can't wait for you to meet my coworkers," but we often tell our coworkers that we are eager to have them meet our spouses or children. If we aren't willing to introduce someone to our spouse, children, parents, or other trusted confidants, there must be a good reason why we feel this way. We'd better find out what that reason is, before admitting that person into our inner circle.

DO THEY JUST LOOK LIKE GOOD GUYS BECAUSE THEY'VE NEVER BEEN TESTED?

Responses to difficult situations, such as having to share resources of time, money, or friends, tell us a great deal about character. How do these folks react when they don't get their way? The point is that many people look like good guys simply because they've never been tested.

If we've never had the opportunity to test the strength of a personal relationship by seeing how the other person reacts to difficult situations, we may not have enough information to fully assess trust. Therefore, we need to take more time before trusting too much, then use the information we've observed to make a more accurate prediction of trustworthiness. Does the person explode, act out-of-control, or verbally abuse us emotionally or physically when things go wrong, or does this person sincerely apologize after a mistake? Does the person we are considering incorporating into our inner circle play the *blame game*? Is everything always our fault? Or, is this person willing to admit he or she makes mistakes, too? It may take longer to get answers to these questions, but avoiding a betrayal is well worth any wait.

DO I GET WHAT I SEE ALL THE TIME?

In a work setting, people often indicated they were looking for self-awareness signals that demonstrated their confidants paid attention to what they said or did, and subsequently understood the effect their actions had on others. When we are at work, we often talk about stability across work and personal lives as being important to trustworthiness. We wonder what people are like outside the workplace and are curious whether people act the same way in their personal lives. But in our everyday, personal lives, we rarely say or think, "I wonder how that person behaves at work." We seem to care about that less. Why? Does this happen because we think of personal life as *real* (who we really are) and work as something less (a bit more fake)? That tells us volumes about how we value personal life and how society teaches us to value work life.

I'm not suggesting that the best data for assessing trustworthy behaviors derives from the workplace. Frankly, neither side gets it completely right, but each has something to offer the other. What follows are the life lessons that have been collected from Chapter 3—insights that we should consider at work.

BE AWARE OF THOSE UNDER TREMENDOUS STRESS

In our personal lives we are careful of trusting too much when our friends/ confidants are under tremendous amounts of stress (experiencing a death, going through a messy divorce, dealing with difficult teenagers). We seem to understand that this added pressure may make our friends act out of character. This was much less of a concern in the workplace, perhaps because we may be less aware of stress in our colleagues than we are in our friends outside the workplace. Most of us tend to conceal our weaknesses/problems in the workplace, as a matter of job preservation. We pretty much expect people to be able to handle and consistently perform under intense pressure at work. It's as if stress has become synonymous with work, and people who can't take the heat should not be in the kitchen. In our work lives, it might be important for us to understand that sometimes people who can't take the heat are *still* in the kitchen and we want to be aware that those who are overly stressed just might be less trustworthy!

NO HARM, NO FOUL

Another familiar theme in personal life, but missing from the workplace, is a confidence that trustworthy confidants won't harm us. We associate the sentence, "She hurt me" with personal settings. Work situations are less personal, less about *me*. We don't think in terms of hurting *me* or helping *me* at work (or at least considerably less so than in personal life). If someone in the workplace said, "He hurt my feelings," we think it's fuzzy; we tell people to toughen up! If this happens in our personal lives, we go after the person who abused our spouse, sister, brother, or we chastise the person who embarrassed our friend in public. The point is that we should associate with those and trust those who won't harm us, in either locale.

SUMMARY OF DIFFERENCES AND SIMILARITIES

The similarities and differences between our criteria of whom to trust in our workplaces and our personal lives are multifaceted. When considering our personal lives:

- We should remember that someone's history is an important predictor of future behaviors; we should use this information to predict future behavior.
- We should also be more results-oriented. Trustworthiness is not a factor of pedigree, looks, or personal wealth. Actions and behaviors alone should influence our assessment of trustworthiness.
- We should ask ourselves if these folks continue to share or not share resources, time, money, or friends. Do they continue to show you the respect of truthfulness even in difficult, stressful situations? Do they show an awareness of how their bad or good behaviors affect you?

When considering our work lives:

- We should withhold trust until we have observed how people respond under duress and have demonstrated consistent trustworthiness in stressful situations.
- We should have more confidence in our trustworthy coworkers.
- We should remember that trustworthy coworkers can help us become good people too.

In general, the important lessons to be learned about trusted work confidants from the Work Trust Rules is that consistency matters, and it matters over time, across people of low status and high status, through good times and bad, and when no one is looking. The major differences between the workplace and home or social situations seem to revolve around the emotional aspects of the relationship.

Most claim it's easier to judge the good guys in the workplace, because our personal lives are filled with added emotion; we want to be loved; we worry about letting loved ones down. At work, or with those we see at our choosing, we can decide to give them a chilly shoulder for a while, or ignore them until we've resolved our inner conflict with them. We call them when we are ready, see them when we have time. In our personal lives, however, we can't *not* see someone with whom we live or share our lives more intimately. Judging good guys in our personal lives can seem more complicated, due to this added emotional layer, but the basic tenets of trustworthiness never change.

Knowing whom to trust may seem obvious and simple, but—it isn't. It takes effort and careful thought to assess someone's trustworthiness. Many of us are reluctant to think about relationships in such a calculating way; however, my research has shown it's essential that we do—otherwise, it's easy to be fooled by the bad guy!

NOTE

1.   https://www.businessinsider.com/theres-a-big-difference-between-your-work-friends-and-your-real-friends-2012-2.

Chapter 5

How Is It That We Fool Ourselves?

The first principle is that you must not fool yourself—and you are the easiest person to fool.

—Richard Feynman

.

T HIS CHAPTER WILL DESCRIBE the ways that we *fool* ourselves into trusting someone who may not be worthy of our trust. Willingness to trust another doesn't operate the same way in everyone. Some people are more willing to trust (sometimes when they shouldn't) and are more easily fooled because they are needier than others. They may perceive few better options in their lives and may have low self-esteem. They set their expectations of good behaviors in others so low that they are willing to fool themselves into accepting bad behaviors as good. They may be so in need of attention that even *bad attention* seems better than none. Anna's story is a good example of these principles.

IF SOMEONE LIES WITH OR FOR ME, THEY ARE PROBABLY LYING *TO* ME

I had been having an affair with a married man for several years. I knew he would never treat me the way he was currently treating his wife—lying, cheating, and sneaking around with me. I just knew I was too special to him. I can't believe how I pretended this was a great sacrifice he was making; he would stay with his wife when, instead, he really wanted to be with me. What I ultimately saw was how much he loved himself and his own personal gain, regardless of the hurt or harm caused to other people, especially me! What I didn't allow myself to see was if someone could be so selfish and thoughtless with his spouse, children, and family, surely he could mistreat me as well when it became convenient for him to do so. He was a real charmer.

When his wife found out about the affair, I was glad. What a surprise to me when he didn't leave her, but instead, left me. Oh, sure, he said all the right things. He gave me the same old story that he just couldn't disappoint his wife and family and leave them to be with me. This time, however, I knew it was just all talk. I knew I had fooled myself long enough. As I look back on that time in my life, I now feel pretty certain that he was seeing other people while he was seeing me. It's pretty clear I wasn't as special as I thought I was. I'm embarrassed and humiliated over the years of my life I gave up because I created a fantasy person in him that never existed. How could I not see who he really was? At the time I was lonely and he took advantage of my loneliness. He was fooling me, but mostly, I was fooling myself, because I was lonely and he made me feel important. That tells you how low my self-esteem was, being with a married man made me feel important. I convinced myself that this married man was noble and honorable, despite his lying and deceitful behaviors. I now know that my behavior shows my own lack of self-respect and self-esteem. While I've learned some important lessons, it's also wrecked my life in so many ways. I find it really hard to trust anyone now—not just men, anyone. And, I'm certain even my closest friends don't trust me; how could they? I've shown them that I will lie and be deceitful to get something I want. I have to live knowing that my close friends must negatively judge my own trustworthiness.

—Anna Thomas, Director of Public Relations[1]

Anna's story is a common one, yet people involved in such relationships often believe their situation to be *unique*. Her catastrophe could have been prevented had she only looked at the obvious signs. Anna now knows she should have not only assessed the married man's behaviors during the time he was with her, but also examined how he treated the supposedly important people in his life. As we'll learn in later chapters, she should have examined her own motivation as well.

We know Anna should have asked herself, "Is someone who puts his personal wants and desires above those of his family, regardless of what he *says*, really worthy of my trust?" This doesn't mean that people in marriages or loving partnerships do not fall out of love and fall in love with someone else. It's the *way* they do this that speaks volumes about their character.

Many of us may have experienced similar situations in our lives, when we learn we have totally misperceived a loving relationship and were so naïve as to believe in someone who betrayed us. We can look to the character of Iago in Shakespeare's *Othello* to further understand such a tragic misperception.

In this play, Shakespeare shows us that trust can be easily abused. Iago's deceptive powers were masterful, creating personal relationships in which few would ever expect *Honest Iago* to manipulate them or use their trusted relationship to accomplish his own selfish agenda. He understood how to use one's shortcomings and what one wanted to believe, to his advantage. Iago was a master of human emotions and behavior. His character illustrates how someone can use our weaknesses (perhaps being too trusting, or needing attention, or being insecure or lonely) to take advantage. This situation parallels Anna's story, in which the married man in Anna's life cloaked his misdeeds in what appeared to be kindness, but used his charm in ways harmful to those around him to serve his own ego.

Our initial reaction to the story above might be, "*Who would allow a known liar into her inner circle of confidants? I can't imagine I would ever trust someone that I knew lied to others. I would never do that.*" Well, more of us make this mistake than we might imagine.

We often know about a person's flaws but have unconscious or illogical reasons to ignore them. We choose to see only what we want to see and not necessarily someone's true character. It isn't that we don't sense the negative nature of deceitful behaviors, but rather that we just choose to overlook them, and our own suspicions, for a personal short-term satisfaction. We consciously don't look at the long-term ramifications of the person's behavior. That was clearly the case with Anna, who admittedly had not been able to find anyone else to share her life. Lonely, she allowed herself to be taken advantage of by someone who cared more for himself than for her—someone who didn't mind hurting his own family and friends for his own short-term gain.

During a recent television broadcast, Oprah Winfrey explained the good-guy concept, as only she can do. In response to a woman in the audience who noted her boyfriend was really a great guy (even though he saw her at his convenience and only on his own terms), Oprah asked, "How do you define good guy? He's a good guy, *but* . . . he's left me waiting for years, he's a good guy *but* . . . I only see him twice a week." She asked, "What does that mean he's a good guy, *BUT* . . . ?"

Oprah's point? If we have to use *but* at the end of our descriptor, he's really not that great a guy. Instead, she told the audience participant that her standards for good were really low, and that a good guy wouldn't treat her that way. Oprah suggested we should all begin to redefine *good*, raise our expectations of *good*, and use the word appropriately, to identify good behaviors, not bad ones. Oprah's comment should make us think about good behaviors in a more systematic way.

How many of us have been guilty of this same kind of faulty logic? We may have a colleague or friend or family member who is a good person, *but* . . . he's bossy, demanding, often rude, never admits to mistakes, *but* he's a good person. Huh?

Here's another bad-guy story of how easily we can fool ourselves, when we want to see something in someone that just isn't there.

Don't Be Afraid of a Background Check

I have had to learn about trust the hard way from my most recent negative life event. I got married last September to my (hopefully very soon-to-be-ex) husband. We dated for nearly two years before we were engaged. Brett had the charm, the degrees, the looks, the salary level, similar level job, and ambition. However, to make a very long story short, I never realized, until after our marriage, when he could not hide things any longer, that he had lied about nearly everything he said and did. He lied to me and his company about receiving his undergraduate and MBA degrees.

He lied about his age, his race (believe it or not), schools he attended, criminal background, women he was seeing, debt he was in, his family, and many other things. Looking back, I realized that it was partially my fault. I realize that since he appeared to have all the qualities that I thought made a "good" guy, I didn't fully check with his family, as I should have. However, he was (and presently is!) an associate VP in a large company, making very good money, and continuing the same lies!

I know that my true story may be a little extreme. However, I realize now, that no matter how great the package looks, I still need to completely check and be definite about one's character, no matter what a "good" guy tells me. Some men and women, no matter how great they seem, are just bad people. So now, my final step in figuring out if I have a good guy or not: "Always do background checks."

Looking back, I realized on many occasions, that I did see signs that he was a very sick person. I just ignored them because it seemed so unbelievable and I was benefiting in many ways. I don't care who you are, and how nice you seem. If we get serious, I'm discreetly doing a background check on you. It's well worth the money.

—Jamie Hayworth, VP, Marketing[2]

Why do we sometimes misjudge others, or why don't we allow ourselves to *see* that we misjudge others? It certainly ties to overlooking or ignoring the warning signs. It certainly entails reassessing and reevaluating the person in question (they are good guys, *but* . . .). It definitely involves taking a look at what we've learned in previous chapters and assessing where we or they went wrong.

My friend and colleague, Professor Al Gini, reminds us that *trust* is a verb, "something that we make, create, build, maintain, and sustain with our actions, promises, commitments, emotions, demeanor, and integrity."[3] This means that actions and behaviors can change over time and we must continually monitor that potential in our relationships. In matters of relationships, we must remember that trust is not fixed or unchanging.

One of the participants in this study explains:

You Can't Judge a Good Guy Using the Standard Metrics

First, I would say that all the standard metrics that were taught to us by our parents don't help. The sleaziest people make great eye contact, have firm handshakes, are steadfast and reliable during the trial period and never, never push too hard. It's the aggregate of their behavior that gives the clues, and the fact that they cannot resist a little bit of exaggeration. Since they know they are sleazy and that they don't really have the "goods," they have the compulsion to extend the truth just a little bit to make sure they are convincing. I let them talk and I listen for inconsistencies, and, if any appear, I question and probe. It usually takes but a few minutes to unroof the phony. Inappropriate familiarity is another good clue.

—Nelson L. Levy, PhD, MD, Chairman and Chief
Executive Officer, The CoreTechs Corporation

Dr. Levy looks for the ways in which untrustworthy people send signals that are dead giveaways about their character. What this tells us is that, fundamentally, we need to know who has our best interests at heart. We need to be able to weed out those with personal agendas that may be harmful to us, our families, close friends, and valued colleagues.

THE BIG TIP

We shouldn't make excuses for bad behavior. When we do, it's clear that our lives are more stressful, less peaceful, and less enjoyable. When assessing whether someone should be trusted as a confidant, especially in our personal lives, condoning bad behavior seems to be the biggest mistake many of us make. Here's what Mary Lou Bechina has to say on the subject:

Don't Make Excuses for Bad Behavior

I'm a pretty good judge of character in the workplace, but in personal relationships, when I like someone, I make excuses for bad behavior. I don't stop to think, I just react. I have always felt like one of the examples in "Smart Women, Dumb Choices."

—Mary Lou Bechina, Former Vice President,
Marketing, Carmichael Leasing Company

Some of us think we're good at telling the good guys from the bad guys at work but do a horrible job of it in our personal lives. This seems to be the case with Bechina. Why is it that we can be so willing to make excuses for someone we like? Why is it that we don't let behaviors speak for themselves, instead of giving negative behaviors more favorable attributes?

"It's OK they didn't call, when they said they would, because they were busy."
No, they were thoughtless.

"It's OK that they lied to me; they didn't want to hurt my feelings."
No, they are liars.

"I know they lie to other people, but they wouldn't lie to me."
No, if they've lied to other people, they've already lied to you.

Bechina understands that her strategy for differentiating good guys from bad guys hasn't worked very well for her, largely because she often makes excuses for people's bad behaviors. She gives them the benefit of the doubt, even when she sees them behaving in ways that signal they are not worthy of her trust. She sometimes takes people too much at face value and then is appalled when they do something bad. Many times, she would have a gut-level feeling that things weren't right, but she would just let it go because she wanted to believe they were good.

As Bechina has learned, this reaction to bad guys, whether they're at work or in social situations, often backfires, leaving the trusting individual angry and hurt about how another person has behaved. Often, the signals were all there. We just chose to ignore them.

Many people I interviewed are like Bechina. They make excuses for people they really want to like. Are women guiltier of this than men? Possibly. Many women set their expectations too low in their more intimate personal relationships. They may inaccurately perceive they have few other options. They may be lonely. They may buy into a cultural norm that suggests women are less valued when they are not attached to a man in some way, even an unhealthy way. These factors can work to create a fantasy perception of their relationships, in which they disregard some essential information about character when deciding if someone is worthy of trust. They want to like someone for all of the wrong reasons and create a mental script that makes everything seem all right. Thus, they set themselves up to be taken advantage of. They fool themselves and, as our introductory quote explained, they are the easiest persons of all to fool. Still, it sometimes happens to all of us.

LIFE'S MULTIPLE CHOICE EXAM

One final way we can be fooled in relationships of trust is through sheer innocence—just simply not knowing or even imagining that people we trust and with whom we have presumably trusted relationships could ever be untrustworthy. I like to compare this to taking a multiple choice exam. In our minds we know that people can do A, B, C, or D. Not being trustworthy, choice *E*, just isn't one of the options. It isn't even in our realm of possibilities. Thus, we are never looking for behaviors that might support that action. Being untrustworthy wouldn't be something you would do to those you love and those who trust you, so you never expect that behavior from your nearest and dearest. People can maintain this level of innocence for a long time. Once they are seriously betrayed, however, *E* becomes a definite possible answer on life's multiple choice exam.

SUMMARY

Now that we know how easy it is to be fooled in our work and personal lives, and know what to look for from work and life lessons, what else can we do to make better assessments of good guys versus bad? We can learn where we fit into the trust-making decision.

NOTES

1. This person's name has been changed to protect anonymity.
2. This person's name has been changed to protect anonymity.
3. Al Gini, *Why It's Hard to Be Good* (New York: Routledge, 2006): 167.

Chapter 6

Where Do *I* Fit into All of This?

A man is at his worst when he pretends to be good.

—Publius Syrius 100 BC

So far we have discussed what to look for when making decisions about whom to trust. But, as the saying goes, it takes two to tango. Accordingly, we need to take a look at our own perspective on trust and see how it might influence our relationships. Understanding the role *we* play in determining whether we find someone trustworthy or not can help us make better trust judgments. First, a few questions to consider:

- How easily can we be influenced by others?
- How easily can we be manipulated by flattery?
- How strong is our propensity to trust others?

HOW VULNERABLE ARE WE TO THE INFLUENCE AND FLATTERY OF OTHERS?

We are all influenced by others to some degree. We can be overly open to influence due to a lack of self-confidence, the need for support or approval, or simply wanting to fit in. Sometimes we allow this, if the situation won't harm us. We're having fun and just don't care. Other times, we permit it because we lack the confidence to speak up for ourselves. In the latter case, we can be talked into doing something we know to be wrong.

Anna, whose story we read in the previous chapter, illustrates the problem of someone who, admittedly, had little self-confidence and self-esteem and was overly influenced by the flattery she received from the married man in her life. Thus, she agreed to do something she knew was harmful to herself and other people. The point is, people with healthy egos and self-esteem are less likely to let others negatively influence them and talk them into behaving badly.

While others' influence can have serious negative effects on our behavior, their influence can also be good. Being vulnerable to the *good* influences of others is a positive trait. As we mature cognitively and emotionally, we can gain a stronger sense of self, allowing us to be less unconsciously negatively influenced by others.

OUR PROPENSITY TO TRUST

Propensity to trust is a measure of how much we would trust someone before we have any information about that person. This has been described as a stable characteristic, one that influences how generally willing we are to trust another.[1] This propensity varies greatly from person to person. Our previous experiences with trusting and untrusting people, our culture, our religion, personality, and family backgrounds all play a role in building our general propensity to trust others.

My own initial propensity to trust people was quite high (probably off the charts) because I came from such a trusting environment. My small town roots, my family, my friends, and the families in the neighborhood where I grew up, created this trusting environment. Over time, however, I've learned that *not* trusting is just as important to a successful work and personal life as is trusting. Thus, assessing our propensity to trust is an important predictor of how willing we will be to trust others.

Let's take a look at the Propensity to Trust Scale (Figure 6.1). The scale is a practical tool in assessing our own propensity to trust. The scale ranges from 1 to 10, with 1 being *totally unwilling to trust* and 10 being *totally willing to trust*.

Let's consider. "Where would you place yourself on the Propensity to Trust Scale, if you had absolutely no information about an individual?" How willing are you to trust a person you meet, even if you have little or no information about this person?

Assume, for example, that a workman is coming to your home. How willing are you to trust that this person will not disturb other items in your home, or will not overcharge you for work that may not really need to be done? Think of someone you have just met—someone you don't know very well. Would

Figure 6.1   Propensity to Trust Scale

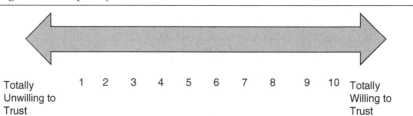

	1	2	3	4	5	6	7	8	9	10	
Totally Unwilling to Trust											Totally Willing to Trust

The higher the number, the more willing you are to trust someone, even without any prior information about the person.

you let them care for your children (if you have any)? Would you allow them into your home if you were not there? How willing are you to trust this person with items or people that you value? Your score might range from being totally unwilling to trust (a score of 1) to totally willing to trust (a score of 10). Where would you place yourself on the Propensity to Trust Scale?

Keep this score in mind, as you begin to systematically assess the trust-worthiness of others and use the other Trust Rules Tools to be introduced in Chapter 9. In that chapter, we'll be systematically assessing behaviors with the Trust Rules Questionnaire. This process will require us to take our time and analyze step by step. To illustrate this, we can turn to Judy Verhave who has developed a system to use when she first meets someone.

EMPLOY CONSTANT TESTING

I start by giving pieces of information, then it's sort of like dating. There are certain places you let somebody in, and over time, you, in essence, build a balance sheet. Once you've got a proven relationship— a lot of chits in the good column—you let them in more.

All relationships are about building trust. So to build trust, there is a constant testing. You get to a plateau where it takes a lot to ruin the relationship. But I never forget—if someone is willing to sell someone else out, they will also be willing to sell me out for their benefit as well.

—Judy Verhave, Executive Vice President, Fidelity Investments

Verhave lets others' actions predict their future behaviors. She *tests, checks, probes, inquires, observes*—powerful verbs that imply action and thinking. What we don't see are the words *gut, feel, emotion*—words that have an intuitive meaning. Verhave understands that determining trustworthiness is a conscious, active process.

The next chapter will provide *us* with these important testing, checking, and probing tools and discuss how telling lies affects our mental and physical health.

NOTE

1.   Roger Mayer, James Davis, and David Schoorman, "An Integration Model of Organizational Trust," *Academy of Management Review* 20 (1995): 20, 709; Robert F. Hurley, "The Decision to Trust," *Harvard Business Review* (September 2006): 716.

Chapter 7

Telling the Truth
about Telling the Truth

I'm not upset that you lied to me; I'm upset that from now on I can't believe you.

—Friedrich Nietzsche

P INOCCHIO, THE WOODEN puppet whose nose grew every time he lied, demonstrates most vividly how lying and being distrustful can affect our physical well-being. While our noses may not grow when we tell a lie, recent research confirms the negative impact of our untrustworthiness, dishonesty, and betrayal on our physical and mental well-being.

Obviously, honesty is one of the best measures of one's trustworthiness, yet 90 percent of people (most of whom self-identify as morally upstanding) would act dishonestly to benefit themselves if they believed they wouldn't get caught.[1] Perhaps this percentage would be different if people understood dishonesty's negative impacts on their mental and physical health, regardless of being caught or not. Because honesty is at the pinnacle of a trusting relationship, it seems important to have a chapter discussing the topic.

TRUST AND OUR MENTAL AND PHYSICAL WELL-BEING

While it may be obvious that lying to friends, spouses, partners, and/or coworkers can negatively affect one's relationships, less obvious is the negative impact that dishonesty can have on one's own well-being. Lying prompts the release of stress hormones, which increases heart rate and blood pressure. Over time, these increases can result in lower-back pain, headaches, diarrhea, stomach issues, and other physical ailments. No doubt when you lie, you feel significant tension in your shoulders, stomach, and/or in other parts of your body, most notably your brain. The longer the lies continue, the more the physical and mental damage.

Consequently, many trust researchers are now asking the question, "Does avoiding lying improve your health?" It seems that lying takes its toll on more than just your relationships. Dr. Anita Kelly, professor of psychology at Notre

Dame, and her colleagues undertook a study that suggests that those who tell fewer lies enjoy significantly better physical and mental health than those who tell more lies.[2]

The 110 adult participants in Dr. Kelly's study were divided into two groups: one group was told to tell no lies in any form, small or large, and a control group that was given no such direction. In order to be certain that both groups were telling the truth about "telling the truth," both groups were given weekly polygraph tests. Major lies, white lies, and exaggerations were measured by the polygraph. Data were collected on both groups for ten weeks. At the end of the study, those in the nonlying group had, on average, seven significantly fewer negative mental and physical stressors (e.g., fewer sore throats, mental tension, headaches, nausea, and signs of depression). Interestingly, even the control group was found to have fewer mental and physical ailments during the weeks that they told fewer major and minor lies. Apparently, all of the stress brought on by telling lies negatively affects our immune systems, causing mental and physical ailments.

Data from the study also showed that those who told fewer lies had improved personal relationships, and their lives generally went more smoothly. Kelly and her colleagues claimed that improved relationships were the factor that most positively affected physical and mental health.

Researcher Sally A. Theran undertook another interesting study examining depressive symptoms and authenticity in 14-year-old boys and girls. There were 435 children in the group.[3] Authenticity was defined as being able to be open and honest in meaningful relationships with parents, peers, and others. Her study found that those who were able to be more authentic and truthful to their parents and peers experienced fewer bouts of depression and anxiety. Being truthful accounted for nearly one-third of the difference in depressive symptoms in girls and nearly one-half of the difference in the boys in the study.

Results of these studies clearly show that lying can add an inordinate amount of stress to one's life and relationships.

SO, WHY DO WE LIE?

Despite the fact that honesty is one of the most important characteristics we can possess, lying can become a bad habit for many people. Over time, those who become experienced liars are not even aware they are lying. Robert Feldman,[4] professor at the University of Massachusetts, Amherst, MA, and author of the book, *The Liar In Your Life*, claims people lie for various reasons. His research shows that men lie to make themselves appear stronger, wiser, and better in general, while women lie to make others feel better. People who are more outgoing and extroverted are more likely to lie than those who are not.[5] Feldman's research shows that people are often surprised to find out that they have been untruthful. When participants in a study were videotaped and then saw the video, they were often surprised to see how many times they had lied.

So then, why do we do it? Why do we lie? We sometimes lie merely to be agreeable and make others feel better. We also lie to make ourselves more important than we really are and we also lie to advantage ourselves over others in some way.

Feldman claims that even little white lies carry a cost, and that the biggest mistakes liars make are lying to themselves:

> When we know we're being dishonest, we feel less trusting about our environment and the people around us. And those little lies create a climate for greater deceptions, leading to *a culture of lies* that pervades today's society.

Dishonesty or betrayal is often a sign of an inability to regulate our emotions or emotional responses. This lack of self-awareness prevents us from thinking through our emotions in the heat of the moment and prevents us from arriving at an understanding of the consequences of our actions. Similar to the discussion in chapters 2 and 3, the all-important variable of self-reflection comes into play. Those who are more capable of self-reflection and of removing their own ego long enough to assess and empathize with the damage their actions will have on their own and on others' futures are less willing to engage in lying behavior.

Another important cause of lying is the inability to delay gratification. We want to get that horrible feeling out of our stomach or wherever else it resides when we've done something we knew was wrong, but we simply can't face the truth. We're caught in a dilemma. It's unbearable to be truthful, yet, as most of us know, the longer-term ramifications of lying our way out of a problem are almost always worse than the actual event itself. Anthony Weiner, Bill Clinton, or John Edwards could attest to that. They wouldn't have seemed nearly as slimy had they been brave enough to tell the truth about their shortcomings. As it is, they made the forgiveness trail even longer!

For Bill Clinton, Anthony Weiner, or John Edwards to lie to their families, the country, and themselves for so long and so egregiously, they had to rationalize the lies as being insignificant, and, in their own minds imagine that the truth would be more harmful to themselves and those around them than the fancy lies they constructed. Needless to say, the same flawed mental decision-making factors that allowed them to engage in their negative behavior in the first place was still in effect, telling them that lying their way out of the problem was the way to go.

Little did they know how wrong they were. It's truly amazing, isn't it, that liars can't seem to learn from the horrible behavior and outcomes of others?

In the class I teach at the University of California Santa Cruz, we have lengthy discussions about white lies, exaggerations, and lying in general. At the beginning of the class, many students argue vehemently that white lies, or small exaggerations, are harmless, and everybody does it. At the end of the class, after they've been studying and reflecting about trust, truthfulness, and its effect on their mental and physical well-being as well as their relationships, the story most often changes. Ask Brian Williams about exaggerations or lies. Brian Williams, an NBC Nightly News TV anchor, whose career, at the time of this writing, is in huge jeopardy due to an exaggeration about his helicopter taking enemy fire while he was covering the war in Iraq, has firsthand knowledge about the effects of exaggerating the truth. Apparently the real story, that a helicopter a couple of hours ahead of his did take enemy fire, wasn't quite juicy enough, thus the exaggeration suggesting that his own helicopter was the one that was in dire danger from enemy fire. This exaggeration has cost Williams a lifetime of trust that was granted by his viewers. Now, his truthfulness is being called into question and he's taking a reprieve from his anchor position. The story will continue, but at the pinnacle of his career with an abundance of wonderful reporting, he will now, most likely, only be remembered for this huge blunder of an exaggeration.

But, back to my UCSC students. Most students, at the end of the quarter claim they feel like different, better people, more centered, more eager to figure out how to be *good guys*. And they most often change their mind about the dangers of telling white lies and exaggerations. I hope the same is true for you.

SO, LET'S GIVE IT A TRY . . . LET'S TAKE THE HONESTY CHALLENGE

It does seem that being honest has positive mental and physical benefits. Most psychologists and counselors claim that we cannot be psychologically sound until we are completely truthful to others and ourselves. It intuitively seems to be so. So, why don't we give it a try? How about taking the Honesty Challenge? Try for one, two, three, or ten weeks to be totally honest in your thoughts, words, and deeds. See for yourself if you have fewer negative mental and physical concerns. See if you feel more centered, more peaceful, and more connected in your relationships at work and at home. You are bound to slip. It will only be natural to do so. When you do, take note of it, and become more and more aware of how often you lie without really thinking of the mental, physical, and relationship ramifications.

The benefits are great. One important thing that occurs when we are more truthful is that we then want to be associated with more truthful, trusting people. We are willing to cut the cord with friends, relatives, and others who are untruthful. It's an ongoing experiment for all of us. The words of the British philosopher Bertrand Russell fit well here:

> Be scrumptiously truthful, even if the truth is inconvenient, for it is more inconvenient when you try to conceal it.

Now, let's venture onto another experiment and examine trust and its relationship to better handling negative emotions in our lives.

NOTES

1.   David DeSteno, "Who Can You Trust," *Harvard Business Review* (March 2014).

2.   Anita Kelly, Presentation, Session 3189, 12 to 12:50 P.M., Room W303C, Level III, Orange County Convention Center. *American Psychological Association's 120th annual convention.* (2012): Saturday, Aug. 4.

3.   Sally A. Theron, "Personality and Individual Differences," *Digit Ratio (2D:4D) and Individual Differences Research* 51 (4) (2011): 423–428.

4.   Robert Feldman, *The Liar in Your Life: The Way to Truthful Relationships* (U.S. Edition: Twelve, 2009).

5.   Ibid.

Chapter 8

Trust, Emotions, and Striving to Reach Resourcefulness

The last of the human freedoms — to choose one's attitude in any given set of circumstances, to choose one's own way.

—*Viktor Frankl*

EMOTIONS. WE EXPERIENCE THEM every day—from joy to anger and everything in between. But do you control your emotions or do they control you? Do you erupt into anger when something doesn't go your way? When you are disappointed in someone or when something negative happens in your life, how do you react? Do your emotions rule you or do you rule your emotions? The answer to this question has a huge impact on how trustworthy other people perceive you to be and how you learn to trust yourself.

Remember one of the predictors of one's trustworthiness, either to others or to yourself: *Likely to respond in a healthy way, when things go wrong.* If others can count on us to be *good* guys only when everything is running along smoothly, then those with whom we work, live, or otherwise share our lives, learn, over time, to not trust us. As I tell my UCSC students, it's really easy to be good when things are going well; it's only the really *good guys* who are good when things aren't going so well. Those are the ones we learn to trust—the "guys" who are good even when things are "bad." Interestingly, we also learn to not trust ourselves when we are only good when it's easy to be good. So, let's try to figure out how we can be better when things aren't going so great, so others will trust us more and we will begin to trust ourselves more as well!

Imagine these scenarios:

You and your new colleague have an important co-sponsored report due tomorrow. It's the first time you've worked with him and you've worked really hard to get your report done on time and in great shape. You are really proud of what you've accomplished. You and your colleague are meeting before heading home tonight, just to be sure the report will be ready to turn in tomorrow. When you go into his office to compare and sync your end products, however, he is still busily retrieving research, writing and scrambling to get his report completed by the tomorrow morning deadline. He asks if you can meet first thing in the morning to sync your two reports into one. You are, naturally, furious with him. If there is something missing in either report, there will be no time in the morning to make important changes. You lose your cool and begin berating your colleague such that everyone in the office can hear your displeasure.

Or you are in a hurry. You have to be somewhere in half an hour and your spouse/partner has mistakenly locked the keys in the car. Of course you are going to feel tension, stress, and maybe even anger. You scream at the person who locked the keys in the car and begin ranting and raving.

But does this screaming and berating the other person help the situation? Does it help you get your reports synced or to your next appointment on time? Or does it merely make a bad situation worse?

Any chance that instead of losing it, you are able to get out of your own ego and attempt to take the perspective of the person who doesn't have the report completed or the person who locked the keys in the car and imagine that they must be feeling pretty crummy about now. You begin to remember that you've done some pretty careless things yourself at times. You remember when you were the cause of someone being late or scrambling at the last minute to get a report completed on time. You remember you had never worked with your new colleague before and realize that you should have checked with him earlier in the week to be certain he was managing his time well and allowing plenty of time for edits and or additions. You realize you probably shouldn't have scheduled the final check-in meeting the night before the report was due, especially when collaborating with someone with whom you had never worked before. And in the case of locking the keys in the car, you realize that if you had gotten ready earlier, there would have been plenty of time to find the spare keys.

Or how about another scenario: You come home from work to discover that your son or daughter has lost the expensive iPad—the Christmas present from just two days ago? Of course you feel anger and disappointment, but how do you react to that anger? Do you explode and reprimand your child in harsh and uncaring ways, so that all your child is really learning is that responding to anger and disappointment in negative ways is appropriate?

Or are you able to imagine how your child might feel? Consider your child's regret at the loss and not being able to play on the iPad again, and, worse yet, knowing that he or she has disappointed you, after promising to be careful with the new, expensive toy. Can you feel angry and allow yourself to be resourceful with that anger? Can you determine a course of action that will teach your child a lesson about being careful with possessions, instead of teaching that anger or disappointment makes it OK to emotionally abuse another person and allow yourself to get out of control emotionally?

Learning to be resourceful with our anger in each of the scenarios above allows us to learn from the experience so that instead of erupting into a cloud of anger, we can have what people are now calling *a teachable moment* for ourselves and for those with whom we've had a conflict.

If you are like me, however, you are feeling stressful just reading these scenarios, and want to learn how to handle yourself better in these anger-inducing moments in which we all are involved from time to time. Remember, when we are better able to manage our emotions, others learn to trust us more and we learn to trust ourselves more as well.

ANGER AND STRESS

Anger and stress are two of our body's reactions to challenging situations. It's simple biology or physiology. When we feel stressful or angry, our sympathetic nervous system is activated. Without a learned intervention, a fight or flight reaction is the result.

Consequently, it's important to remember that our emotions are neither positive nor negative, but rather instinct-based responses to environmental stimuli that cause physical, biochemical changes and feelings in our body. Emotions just exist—they occur without thought or action on our part. You can't avoid them. You will feel anger or fear at times. It's natural and instinctive to do so. But without some conscious management of this instinct-based process, your reaction to these stimuli can be mentally and physically harmful.[1] We lose the trust of those we love and care for, and we also lose faith in our own trustworthiness.

WE CAN LEARN HOW TO DO IT BETTER

It's important to remember that not all stress is negative. Some stress is helpful, and, like many things in life, levels of appropriate stress follow the bell curve; that is, we all need some level of stress to improve, grow, and develop in meaningful ways. Some level of stress helps us be better on the basketball court, in our boardrooms, on our jobs, and with our friends and family. When there's too much stress in our lives, however, that's when we need to learn to manage stress in more mentally and physically healthy ways.

Fortunately, one of the blessings of our human development over the rest of the animal kingdom is that we *can* learn more physically and mentally healthy ways of dealing with negative emotions. The key concept here is that managing our negative emotions in healthy ways is a learned behavior. This conscious awareness can be learned by thoughtful feedback from parents, friends, teachers, ourselves, or others who are willing to attend to our development in thoughtful ways. Most often we learn a physical reaction to anger from our families, or from those who raised us. Then, if we learned a good lesson, we attempt to repeat it. If, instead, we had poor role models, we can spend a lifetime trying to retrain ourselves to better manage negative emotions and stress.

There are three kinds of stress, each damaging our physical and/or mental health in direct ways:

- physical (you are injured in some way),
- chemical stress (you are taking in too much alcohol or too many drugs, either prescription or recreational),
- emotional stress (you haven't learned to deal with your emotions in healthy ways).

This chapter is concerned with learning to manage emotional stress. As noted above, emotional stress is greatest when we haven't learned to deal with our emotions in healthy ways. Emotional stress can also result from attempting to keep negative emotions at bay, by suppressing the emotion and not allowing ourselves to be present and aware of the fear, the anger, or whatever emotion we are experiencing. Particularly for young boys and men, "Be tough!" "Don't show you are afraid!" "Don't cry!" are repeated mantras throughout their lives. Boys learn this early and, as men, they often suppress fear, exchanging it for anger, which is considered more culturally appropriate for men and boys.

While it tends to be more culturally acceptable for women to overtly express their emotions, they are also often criticized for any open displays of emotion that cross some invisible boundary. Remarks such as, "You're too sensitive" "You're crazy" "Are you PMSing?" can cause women to feel guilty about their emotional responses. Both men and women, early in their lives, learn to either suppress or feel guilty about their emotions, with potentially serious physical and emotional consequences.

THE SOLUTION

We have three choices when faced with negative emotions:

1. Fight—lash out at someone or something
2. Flight—leave the situation or problem (Run from it)
3. Or the best option—do nothing and stay present in the emotion

When we react to an emotion, such as anger, with fight (hurting someone else) or flight (suppressing the emotion by running away from a problem), we train ourselves over time to not really feel the emotion, and thus continue patterns of negative behaviors that are harmful to others and often ourselves. So, in the examples given above of a colleague being late with their part of a report, or a spouse/partner locking the keys in the car, or a son or daughter losing the iPad after only two days, it's not healthy to *not allow* yourself to feel the emotion of anger. The key is to respond to the anger/stress in more healthy ways. This, in essence, is something we practice, learn, and hopefully get better at over time.

So, to the extent that we can be conscious of our negative emotions, we can use them to our success and turn negative emotions into a state of *resourcefulness*, which is managing the instinctual responses to emotions, such as fear or anger, in such a way that the individual becomes *proactive* rather than *reactive*. This proactivity allows for resourcefulness and is a learned behavior. In fact, many claim that the most effective and successful people have a restored and connected relationship with their emotions.

Thus, the healthy way to deal with an emotion, such as anger, is to allow ourselves to *sit* with it by observing the anger, even asking ourselves where within our bodies we are feeling the anger. We may experience that anger in our shoulders, stomach, back, head, or other specific body part. Allowing ourselves to feel where the negative emotion resides in our bodies might also allow us to restore ourselves to equilibrium with a socially acceptable alternative. We do not ignore the emotion or alter the emotion to a new form (e.g., turn fear into anger). We instead deal with the physical manifestation of that emotion. Can we imagine being able to retrain ourselves to feel the emotion of anger and train ourselves to relax when we feel the emotion of anger or fear? Can we imagine that these instinctive emotions would happen and yet have little negative impact on our behavior and our lives? This new behavior would be *trust-building* in ourselves and others.

SOME ALTERNATIVES

So, what are these alternatives that can help us reduce our anger response and better understand the other person's perspective? Remember, we can train our brain and our mental script to make better choices when in difficult situations. In order for our brain and mental script to be top-performing, however, we must get the rest we need, eat the balanced diet we should, stay hydrated, and get the exercise needed to be mentally and physically healthy. When we aren't attending to the health and well-being of our physical bodies, it is more likely we can/will react poorly in a challenging situation.

Give it a try. When was the most recent time you became angry? Can you recall where the anger resided within your body? Did your shoulders tighten up? Did your stomach feel achy and sick? Did you have tension in your legs or feet? Did it cause you to have a headache or a stressful feeling in your head? The next time you feel angry, fearful, or stressed (remember, most stress is merely "fear" of something), try to determine what that *something* is that you are fearful of and which is forcing you to become angry. Try to recall where the anger manifested itself within your body. If you are able to assess the presence of anger and determine the physical manifestation, you can then eventually train yourself to apply a healthy physical response to the manifestation and allow yourself to become *resourceful* with that negative emotion.

Table 8.1   Suggested Alternative Responses to a Physical Response to an Emotion

Physical Manifestation	Suggested Alternative Action
Head	Sleep, massage, talking with friend, parent, someone you trust, meditation, deep breathing, hydrate
Back	Yoga, massage, long walk, more rest, deep breathing, hydrate
Stomach	Healthy meal, breathing exercises, green tea, hydrate
Shoulders/Chest	Massage, arm exercises, yoga, meditation, deep breathing, hydrate

BECOMING RESOURCEFUL

When we stay present in our emotion, we become trustworthy and thoughtful, as we have an awareness of the repercussions and consequences of our behavior. We become self-reflective. Being aware of our emotions allows us to use them in more positive ways. Drugs, excessive alcohol, fighting, or flight are often used to mask our emotions. When we stay present and do not go into the past (carry our baggage around with us), or project ourselves into the future (worry about what might happen), we can stay in full consciousness where we have all of our resources available to us and we can become *resourceful*.

As soon as we move away from the present and a state of awareness we can easily slip into *protective* mode, where we emotionally regress and do whatever we can to just survive the negative emotional state, often resorting to the fight-or-flight response. The ability to experience the emotion and stay present, even when that emotion is uncomfortable, leads to a state of resourcefulness and freedom of choice (as the Frankl quote at the beginning of this chapter suggests) rather than being a slave to a more primitive instinctual response. Being in a state of resourcefulness and freedom allows better adaptation to the environment, and better adaptation is one way we can define healthy mental and physical well-being. As we become better at managing the instinctual emotional responses in various situations, our level of self-assurance and self-trust increases. We learn that we can stay in a state of resourcefulness in spite of fearful environmental situations.

For me, it's not about just surviving. It's about asking the question, "How can I help myself and others live better, less stressful, and more peaceful lives?" It's a main reason I've written this book. So, why don't we allow ourselves to be courageous and allow ourselves to feel anger, fear, or other emotions without reacting negatively to them? When we do, we begin the journey of learning that we are capable of being more trustworthy to ourselves and to others. As we become better and better at managing the primitive instinctual response to stressors and become more self-assured with more self-trust, we are able to extend that trustworthy state beyond ourselves to others. And that's living the best life possible!

Now that we've examined how we can be fooled, how lying affects our mental and physical health, and how to better manage our emotions so we can be more trustworthy to ourselves and better know whom we can and can't trust, let's return to our systematic assessment of telling the good guys from the bad guys in work and life. Let's take a look at the Trust Rules Toolkit in Chapter 9.

NOTE

1.   Thanks to Dr. Randal Johnson, "Our Emotions and Trust," Lecture for UCSC students in "Trust Rules" class, Fall 2014. Many of the ideas in this chapter come from his significant lecture to the students in my "Trust Rules" class at UCSC.

Chapter 9

Using the Trust Rules Toolkit

If you think there is good in everybody, you haven't met everybody.

—Anonymous

THE PROPENSITY TO TRUST SCALE, used in the previous chapter, is part of the Trust Rules Toolkit developed for this book. The Trust Rules Toolkit includes:

1. The Propensity to Trust Scale, used in the previous chapter to assess our own propensity to trust;

2. The Trust Rules Questionnaire that assesses our perceptions of another's trustworthiness;

3. The Trust Rules Scale that assesses the relative ratings of our current and potential confidants;

4. The Trust Rules Self-Questionnaire, to be introduced in Chapter 20, which assesses our own trustworthiness;

5. A How Trustworthy Are You Scale, also to be introduced in Chapter 20, which assesses the relative weighting of our own trustworthiness.

You can find a copy of each of these items at the end of this book. We will work with the Trust Rules Self-Questionnaire and the Trust Rules Self-Scale later in Chapter 20.

We have now arrived at one of this book's goals, which is to provide more objective measures for evaluating trustworthiness. Through the interviews I've undertaken and introspection about my own experiences with trust in the workplace and in my personal life, I have generated a great deal of information and data. How do we put this data into a meaningful and useful model?

If we think back to each insight in Chapters 2 and 3, we'll see that we've captured a characteristic of a good guy (a trustworthy person) that is an actual measure of a person's trustworthiness. This characteristic is now part of the Trust Rules Questionnaire (Table 9.1). Let's begin by learning just how to use that questionnaire.

Table 9.1 Trust Rules Questionnaire

Select a potential or current confidant. Respond to each questionnaire on a scale of 1-10, with 1 indicating the person **does** not have this characteristic and 10 meaning this person **does have** this characteristic. Place the number you have selected in the space provided at the beginning of each question. The sum of the numbers is the Total Score. The higher the number, the more trustworthy you perceive this person to be.

Value	Trait	Definitely Does Not Have Characteristic							Definitely Has Characteristic		
	This person has a history that demonstrates good values.	1	2	3	4	5	6	7	8	9	10
	This person is likely to respond in a healthy way, when things go wrong.	1	2	3	4	5	6	7	8	9	10
	This person admits and learns from mistakes.	1	2	3	4	5	6	7	8	9	10
	This person has a self-awareness of how his/her behavior affects others.	1	2	3	4	5	6	7	8	9	10
	This person treats everyone the same, regardless of level in the hierarchy (work or social).	1	2	3	4	5	6	7	8	9	10
	This person demonstrates consistent good behavior.	1	2	3	4	5	6	7	8	9	10
	This person has positive qualities, other than just good looks, a good education, and wealth.	1	2	3	4	5	6	7	8	9	10
	This person never takes advantage of others with his/her own good looks, education, or wealth.	1	2	3	4	5	6	7	8	9	10
	This person admits when he/she doesn't know something.	1	2	3	4	5	6	7	8	9	10
	This person demonstrates absolute integrity.	1	2	3	4	5	6	7	8	9	10
	This person genuinely considers others in his/her life.	1	2	3	4	5	6	7	8	9	10
	This person voluntarily, in useful ways, tells me when I do something wrong.	1	2	3	4	5	6	7	8	9	10
	This person helps me to be a better person.	1	2	3	4	5	6	7	8	9	10
	I would introduce this person to my family and other trusted confidants.	1	2	3	4	5	6	7	8	9	10
	This person responds in a healthy way, when he/she doesn't get his/her way.	1	2	3	4	5	6	7	8	9	10
	This person holds him/herself to the same standards he/she established for others.	1	2	3	4	5	6	7	8	9	10
	This person does the right thing.	1	2	3	4	5	6	7	8	9	10
	This person sticks by others in bad/tough times.	1	2	3	4	5	6	7	8	9	10
	This person speaks the same of everyone, whether in their presence or not.	1	2	3	4	5	6	7	8	9	10
	This person is likely to share resources (time, space. money, friends).	1	2	3	4	5	6	7	8	9	10

___ **TOTAL SCORE (Total possible score between 20 and 200)**

HOW TO BETTER ASSESS OTHERS

Select someone whose trustworthiness you'd like to assess. Think of a boss, friend, or someone you know very well (you'll do this test on yourself later!). We'll use the Trust Rules Questionnaire to assess the trustworthiness of that person. There are twenty questions in the Trust Rules Questionnaire, each ranging in value from 1 to 10, with 1 being the lowest possible score for each question. Thus, the potential Total Scores for those you are assessing can range from 20 to 200. Now, proceed through the following steps:

Step 1. Read and answer, in order, each of the questions in the Trust Rules Questionnaire. Example: "Does this person have a history that demonstrates good values?" Rate the person on a scale of 1–10, with 1 being "definitely does not have this characteristic," and 10 being "definitely does have this characteristic." Score each question, placing the appropriate number on the line provided at the beginning of each question. Be sure to respond objectively to each question based on that person's *observed* behaviors and actions and NOT how you may *feel* about this person. Use actions and behaviors ONLY to make your assessment. It can be easy to fall into a trap of rationalizing a person's behaviors; don't do it. Just respond to each question from a behavior and action point of view. If you don't know someone well enough to rate each one of these items, that alone is useful information. Don't fully trust this person until you get that information!

Step 2. When you reach the bottom of the Trust Rules Questionnaire, add up the total number of points to arrive at the Total Score.

Step 3. Based on the Total Score from Step 2, situate this person on the Trust Rules Scale (Figure 9.1) somewhere between the parameters of Very Trustworthy (a highest possible score of 200) to Very Untrustworthy (a lowest possible score of 20). The Trust Rules Scale will show you a rank-ordering of your relationships, based on each person's trustworthiness.

Step 4. Continue to rate each person whose trustworthiness you want to measure.

If a friend or confidant receives a high score on each of the questions on the Trust Rules Questionnaire, you have a good guy!

Figure 9.1   Trust Rules Scale

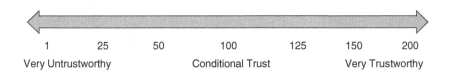

| 1 | 25 | 50 | 100 | 125 | 150 | 200 |

Very Untrustworthy   Conditional Trust   Very Trustworthy

Based on the Total Score from the Trust Rules Questionnaire, place your current or potential confidant on the Trust Rules Scale. The more positive characteristics, and the higher the number on the Trust Rules Questionnaire, the more you can trust this person.

QUANTIFY THE DIFFERENCES

Once we've used the Trust Rules Questionnaire to measure our potential or current confidant's trustworthiness, we may find this person isn't as trust- worthy as we thought (when we used our *intuition* or *gut* to make that determination). The Trust Rules Questionnaire is a system that allows us to quantify trustworthy differences in more useful ways. While the ranking system will be unique to our own perceptions, the ranking will serve as our own relative measure of the trustworthiness of each of our confidants or potential confidants.

After we have obtained each score, we can then make better decisions about whom we can and cannot trust and decide whether our relationships with these individuals should change or remain the same. The Total Score on the Trust Rules Questionnaire can help us assess whom to include in our inner circle of confidants and can also help us build better relationships by identifying weak links. If we discover a weak area, we can then assess its importance and determine if we must limit our interactions with that individual in important ways. No one is perfect (more on this later) and it's up to each one of us to decide what level of imperfection we are willing to live with.

For example, if someone's Total Score on the Trust Rules Questionnaire allows you to place that person near 200 on the Trust Rules Scale, you know you can have an unconditional trust relationship with this person, a relationship that would be trustworthy regardless of time, place, or circumstances, and you will know this with a high degree of confidence. This person can be considered an unconditional trusted confident.

However, untrustworthy relationships, those in which we should never trust the other person, are those whose Total Score on the Trust Rules Questionnaire forces you to place them on the lower end of the Trust Rules Scale. Those on the lowest end of the scale should *never* be considered trusted confidants, regardless of how charming or charismatic they may be. Think about why they score low. Has your intuition ever signaled to you what this more objective analysis signals?

NEED MORE INFORMATION?

In some cases, we may find we are unable to answer, with confidence, all of the questions about each of our potential confidants. We may need more information about some people in order to complete the Trust Rules Questionnaire. This is an indication for us to use the questions to probe our relationships further and to gather the necessary information before admitting this person into our inner circle. This doesn't mean the person is unworthy of our trust; it just means that we do not yet have sufficient information to make a judgment.

While totally trustworthy (our trusted confidants) and totally untrustworthy (never to be considered trusted confidants) relationships are at the extreme ends of the trust continuum, the vast majority of our relationships are *conditional* relationships. We might place someone on the untrustworthy end of the continuum simply because we do not yet have enough information to fully evaluate this person's trustworthiness. Or, we may place most in the middle because we have incomplete data. We might also place someone in the middle because we trust that person, but only in specific situations. Few people we know will be at the extremes on the continuum. Most of our relationships are those that have *conditions* under which we can assume they would be more or less trustworthy.

For example, for Andrew Housser there are certain conditions under which he would either trust or distrust someone:

> For some, I trust that they would not steal or do anything dishonest in my absence, etc. This is someone I could leave in charge of the office when Brad, my Founding Partner and Co-CEO, and I are out of the office. It is often small actions that create or limit that kind of trust. For example, some people are always trying to slip through the cracks or get away with minor things that are not necessarily dishonest, but certainly create a subconscious feeling of distrust that would prevent me from placing unconditional trust in that person.
>
> Then, there is trust in knowing that things will get done; that is, when I ask them to get something done, I know it will happen.
>
> These two types of trust are not necessarily related. There are some people I have complete confidence that when I tell them to do something it will get done, but these are not necessarily the same people I would trust to be in the office alone. The opposite is true as well.
>
> Andrew Housser, Founding Partner and Co-CEO,
> Freedom Financial Network

Housser presents a perfect scenario that describes the importance of understanding that some relationships have *conditions* under which they are or are not trustworthy.

Let's look to the next chapter to learn more about how to live and work with these conditional trust relationships, those *not-quite-so good guys.*

Chapter 10

Those Conditional Trust Relationships

It's funny how sometimes the people you'd take a bullet for, are the ones behind the trigger.

—Ritusagoo

IN THE PREVIOUS CHAPTER we discussed the continuum of trust and learned that some people may be trusted or distrusted *unconditionally*. But what about those folks we've only known a short while or under limited circumstances? Until we have sufficient information to assess these potential new members of our inner circle, these relationships will fall into the *conditional* trust bucket; the not-so-sure-if-you're-a-good-guy bucket. Or what about those who fall in the center of the Trust Rules Scale—those with whom we have less than perfect trusting relationships? Moving these folks from a level of *conditional* trust to *trustworthy* or *untrustworthy* status requires that we assess two important factors: whether or not we have a set of common goals and the strength or weakness of the situation.

WE BOTH WANT THE SAME OUTCOMES

Conditional relationships can be trustworthy when the goals of each party are aligned—when we both want the same outcomes. Sound complicated? Let me explain.

Imagine that we are involved in a team-oriented work project in which everyone is rewarded based on the productivity of the team. Taking into consideration everyone's individual ability to accomplish the task, we can be confident, with a high degree of probability, the team members will work to reach the goals and be trustworthy in their commitments. The team shares a common goal and common reward for doing so; the incentive to perform well has a strong individual component. Remember Adam Smith: "The individual pursuit of happiness accrues to the common good?" Well, what Smith could have said was, "The individual pursuit of happiness accrues to the common good, *if our goals are aligned*!" If they aren't aligned, look out! This guy may not be trustworthy. So, if we find ourselves working with someone who didn't do so well on the Trust Rules Questionnaire, this person could be considered more trustworthy, *if* he or she desires the same outcome we do. Examples: Warren may be slimy, but if we both want Sue to get the job, we can work together to make it happen. Your brother-in-law might be a deceitful so-and-so, but if you both want to sell mom and dad's old car, you can work together to make it happen. However, if your untrustworthy brother-in-law doesn't want to sell mom and dad's old car and you do, or Warren wants someone to get the job other than Sue, look out! You probably can't trust either one of them out of your sight!

However, those who scored as Totally Trustworthy on the Trust Rules Questionnaire probably wouldn't change their behavior much at all. That's why we want to find these good guys; they are good in nearly every situation! This doesn't mean that trustworthy people will agree with every one of your goals. What it does mean is that when your goals differ, the trustworthy person will treat you with respect during the resolution of those conflicts.

This is true both in our personal and our work lives. Those with whom we have conditional relationships (aren't fully trustworthy, as noted by the Trust Rules Questionnaire) change their behavior as their goals change. As a valued colleague of mine says, *"Their position changes as their position changes."* With relationships of this nature, we learn that trust depends on the alignment of goals. When our goals are aligned, the other person will interact with us as a trusted confidant. When our goals are not aligned, the other person may interact as a rival. Thus, we must never assume this goal-aligned relationship is anything more than it is. We should never reveal important confidences to people we categorize in this way, for when the alignment of goals has ended, the confidant can just as easily become our rival. To further complicate the matter, the confidant-turned-rival can again appear to be our trusted confidant, should the goals once again be aligned.

The story below, recounted by a well-published author, is another illustration of a conditional relationship gone awry.

It's Easy To Be Duped When You Don't Have Enough Information

The editor with whom I worked on my last book contract decided to leave the publishing company with which I had the contract. Prior to his decision to leave the publishing firm, he was extremely friendly, gave me tons of time, had great ideas—was just my best friend. I, of course, thought this was very sincere, and thought we were building a relationship that was beyond just the book (i.e., we both enjoyed each other's thinking, etc.)—that his friendship wasn't just because our goals were aligned. I spoke with him a few days before he left the company (he left within a week), and I couldn't believe he was the same person. He was not only preoccupied, but very rude, saying he didn't have the time to talk with me and that he would give me the name of someone else to call.

I was very disappointed in him, but in retrospect, mostly disappointed in myself that I hadn't realized I had not had enough interactions with this person to make a trust-related judgment. Had I allowed myself to objectively think about this I would have realized that he was so helpful to me because our goals were aligned; nothing more, nothing less. It was easy to be duped because I didn't have enough information!

—Donna Samuels,
Internationally Recognized Author[1]

This story shows how easy it is to miscategorize a relationship; most often those miscategorized relationships are *conditional* relationships. As with the author above, this happens often when someone is benefiting from us in some way. The person can be flattering and attentive because he or she wants something from us (our time, resources, our own attention, or advice). We can easily be duped, because the flattery and attention are so seductive.

Conditional relationships change, based on the circumstances at the time, and our interaction with these people should reflect the tentativeness of that relationship. Therefore, we shouldn't say or do anything during the alignment period we may regret, as they may once again become rivals or people with whom we choose to no longer associate. When we are no longer their confidant, it's common that they *spill the beans* and tell all we have told them under the guise of confidence.

Another important condition to consider when we have less-than-perfect trusting relationships is what social psychologists refer to as the strength/weakness of the situation.

LOOK AT THE STRENGTH OR ABSENCE OF CONTROLS IN THE SITUATION

When someone falls into the conditional trust column (scored somewhere in the middle or lower end on the Trust Rules Questionnaire), it's important to also consider the situations in which this person will be interacting and the situations in which we will interact with them, before assessing their trustworthiness. Research has shown that we can be more successful at predicting behaviors if we remember there are strong and weak situations that could affect how one behaves in a conditional trust relationship.

In my interview with Randy Cohen, the *New York Times Magazine* columnist, Cohen noted that over time he has changed his opinion about the influence of one's character on behavior. Cohen claimed:

> What I've come to think more and more is that character counts for less and less and what most influences our behavior is the situation in which we find ourselves.

For Cohen, the situation in which we find ourselves is a far better predictor of how we will behave and the ethical or unethical choices we will make.

For social psychologists, a strong situation is one in which everyone would behave in nearly the same way. For example, we may be in a classroom, or a training session, or a lecture of some kind. In this setting, it's highly probable that most would listen, remain quiet, and pretty much behave quite similarly. We can trust, with a high degree of certainty, that nearly everyone will remain polite and respectful of others in that strong situation.

In contrast, a weak situation is one in which there are weaker social and cultural signals that tell us how to behave and in which we are free to decide for ourselves how we choose to act.[2] Examples might include attending our neighbor's fiftieth birthday party, the office holiday party, a bachelor or bachelorette party, or going on a business trip with someone of the opposite sex or even the same sex, if this includes a possibility of betraying a partner. In these instances, deciding on appropriate behavior is much more an individual choice. Consequently, one's character plays a greater role in predicting behavior in these weak situations, situations in which behavioral norms are not clearly defined.

In the absence of these social controls, those people with whom we have strong, trusting relationships (those who score high on the Trust Rules Questionnaire) do not change behavior dependent on the strength or weakness of the situation. Contrastingly, those with whom we have conditional trust relationships (those who scored lower on the Trust Rules Questionnaire) may alter their trustworthiness, based on whether or not someone is monitoring their behavior or whether the situation leaves little room for discretionary choices (e.g., sitting in a classroom, driving down the road).

One's true character is more likely to surface in situations where cultural and social rules are less well defined, so we should be more observant of the ways people act in these situations. Also, in situations where expected behaviors are less well defined, we would be less likely to trust those we have placed in a conditional trust category (those who scored lower on the Trust Rules Questionnaire). The work and personal life insights from Chapters 2 and 3 remind us that those who are most trustworthy are consistent in their behaviors. They are not just trustworthy when the situation makes it easier to be so.

The bottom line is that it is important to our personal and work-related success that we appropriately categorize our relationships with those people with whom we interact. It is also important to periodically *reassess* those we trust, as people and situations can change over time.

SO, HOW DO I BETTER ASSESS OTHERS?

The strategies covered in this chapter can be applied both at work and in our personal lives to systematically assess our close colleagues/confidants and to develop a continuum of trustworthy to untrustworthy relationships, based on valid data. As we compare the behaviors of those already in our inner circle, or those we might wish to allow into our inner circle, the decision about whom to trust and whom not to trust should be by design (thoughtful) and not by default (unconscious). The Trust Rules Toolkit from Chapter 9 will help you make these thoughtful decisions.

Now that we have learned about conditional trust relationships and can avoid being duped by trusting relationships based on strong and weak situations or goal alignment, let's examine how we can build more trusting relationships in our families.

NOTES

1.   This person's name and affiliation have been changed to protect anonymity.

2.   Linda Stroh, Gregory Northcraft, and Margaret Neale, *Organizational Behavior: A Management Challenge* (New Jersey: Lawrence Erlbaum Associates, 2002).

Chapter 11

Building Trust in Our Families

A family is a bunch of people who keep confusing you with someone you were as a kid.

—Robert Brault

By NOW, IT MUST BE pretty clear to you that learning whom you can and can't trust and how to be a trustworthy person yourself is a lifelong journey. Fortunately, the *Trust Rules* in this book can speed up the process significantly. It might also be helpful to understand what's behind the process of learning to trust and to becoming trustworthy ourselves. Let's take a look at what the experts have learned and see how to apply their findings to our own lives. As a bonus, we'll end this chapter by learning some family mechanics that can help us teach our children to be more trustworthy, too. Let's start, then, at the beginning.

Between birth and 18 months of age, there is a developmental stage that we must all master if we are to become trustworthy adults. That crucial information comes from the work of Erik Erikson, a world-renowned 20th-century social psychologist. So, is the ability to assess trustworthiness something we must learn or is it present at birth?

THE YALE BABY LAB

Research by Dr. Karen Wynn from Yale University's Baby Lab challenges the perspective that we arrive in this world as a blank slate, and her research adds important information to this debate. Dr. Wynn has been studying babies for many years and was the principal psychologist on the research team whose findings show that babies have a real sense of good and bad that seems to be inherent. In fact, at three months, babies are already formatted with a moral code and the ability to tell the difference between good guys and bad guys, and, when given the opportunity, they choose to be with the good guys. How did the researchers discover this? They used puppets. In one of the now-famous studies, babies as young as three months old viewed a puppet show in which a cat puppet attempts to open a box, and is helped in this task by a bunny puppet (colorfully identified). Another bunny dressed differently from the first bunny, sits on the box, preventing the cat from opening it. Later, when presented with both the good bunny and the bad bunny, the babies overwhelmingly reached for the good bunny puppet. In fact, 80 percent of six-month-olds and 90 percent of three-month-olds chose the good bunnies instead of the bad bunnies.

In another puppet show conducted by the Baby Lab, a colorfully clad puppet attempts to climb a hill. At times a second puppet helps the climbing puppet and at other times another puppet, differently dressed, attempts to thwart the climbing puppet's efforts. After the puppet show is over, the baby is shown both the helpful and unhelpful puppets. Once again, the babies overwhelmingly choose the good guy puppet. The babies continue to exhibit a distinct preference for the kind puppets by staring at the good puppet for a significantly longer time than they stare at the evil puppet. This research from the Yale Baby Labs highly suggests that we are preprogrammed to tell the difference between the good guys and the bad guys.

A DEAL WITH THE DEVIL

An interesting follow-up to these studies, also conducted by the Yale Baby Lab, is called "A Deal with The Devil." The research question in this study asks, "Just what does it take for us to interact with bad guys?"

The babies again watch a puppet show in which good and bad puppets perform. After the show is over, each puppet (good and bad) offers the baby some crackers. The good puppet offers the baby one cracker, but at the same time the bad puppet offers the baby two crackers. Invariably, the babies choose the good puppet. The researchers claim that this study shows that babies are even willing to make a sacrifice (of one less cracker) to associate with the good puppet.

But, when the study design is changed a bit and the good puppet still only offers one cracker, but the bad puppet now offers the baby eight crackers, two-thirds of the babies choose the bad puppet's crackers. So, what does this all mean? Dr. Wynn claims it means that if you are a bad guy, the only way to get good guys to associate with you is if you have more resources; thus, there seems to be a cost associated with being a bad guy. Even babies are able to tell the difference, but if you have enough "goodies," we *will play* with you.

Dr. Wynn also claims that it is very hopeful, however, that one-third of the babies still choose the fewer crackers from the good guy puppet. She suggests that if even babies can override a selfish instinct to reward a good guy, there is hope for all of us adults.[1]

Does this sound familiar to you? Are you willing to spend time with people you may not really like or care for or who you think aren't really good people just because they have more resources of some kind? Ask yourself if you would still associate with the bad guys if they didn't have as much money or other resources. Gut check time!

So, if we know that we may have an innate ability to separate good guys (trustworthy) from bad guys (untrustworthy) early in our lives, what causes us to become less trustworthy (bad guy) or more trustworthy (good guy) over time?

TRUST MATTERS

The Stanford Marshmallow Study (Yes! Marshmallow Study!) has important input into this question.[2] This was a longitudinal study, which means the same children were part of the study throughout their lives. Previous studies have shown that children who are better able to delay gratification are more successful in both their personal and work lives later in life. The Stanford studies also measured children's ability to delay gratification, and their results confirmed what earlier researchers had found. Children who were better able to delay gratification were more successful in both their work and personal lives.

Here's how the study was conducted. Children ages 4 to 6 were placed in a room and offered one marshmallow. The researcher told the children that if they could wait until the researcher returned (approximately 15 minutes later), they would be rewarded with another marshmallow. The choice was theirs: wait or eat now. While few of the children ate the marshmallow right away, only one-third were able to wait the entire 15 minutes to get the second marshmallow. In longitudinal follow-up studies, the children who were able to wait the 15 minutes for the additional reward were shown to have better personal and work lives. They had higher SAT scores, better educations, less substance abuse, and even better body mass index and other measures.

While the famous Stanford Marshmallow Study has been the guiding influence of our understanding of children's ability to maintain self-control, follow-up studies have shown interesting links between behavior and trust. One such study was conducted at Rochester University.[3] In this study, one group of children were promised that the researcher would return with more, better, bigger crayons if they could wait before using the small number of crayons they had just been given. When the researcher returned, the children were told, sorry, but they couldn't have more, better, bigger crayons. This was identified as the unreliable group.

Those children in the other, reliable group were given the expected bigger, better crayons when the researcher returned. The children in the unreliable group were also then subsequently told they would be given a sticker and that, if they could wait and not use the sticker, the researcher would return with more and better stickers. When the researcher returned, they once again told this group of children in the unreliable group that there were no more stickers to be given. In the reliable group, however, the researcher, as promised, returned with the expected bigger and better stickers.

The Marshmallow Study procedures we discussed above were then reenacted. Children were given one marshmallow and told that, if they could wait, they would be rewarded with an additional marshmallow. The choice was theirs: wait for a reward of one more marshmallows or eat the one marshmallow now.

The children who were in the unreliable group waited, significantly, four times less to eat the marshmallow than did those children in the reliable group. The lead professor on this follow-up study, Dr. Richard Aslin, Professor of

Brain and Cognitive Sciences at Rochester University, claims the broad implications from this follow-up study suggest that children who live in environments where long-term gains are nonexistent form weak trust bonds. They
learn to act more impulsively and make short-term gain behavior choices.
For those children who learn that long-term gains do exist, the trust bond is
strong, and they learn better self-control and to act less impulsively.

Thus, it seems that at very young ages we are fully capable of accessing
information from our environment and experiences and calculating a cost/
benefit analysis of whether we should trust that someone will fulfill our promises or not. If, over time, we learn they will not, we learn to act accordingly and
behave in the short term. If, however, we learn that we can trust what someone
says and promises, we learn to delay gratification and behave in the longer
term and less impulsively.

SO, HOW DO WE DO IT—HOW DO WE RAISE MORE TRUSTWORTHY CHILDREN?

After reading the results and implications from these interesting studies, we
might begin to wonder how to do a better job of fostering trust in our own
children. The answers are actually quite simple and obvious. Think before you
make promises. When you do promise something, follow through. Trust is
earned. This applies to both positive and negative consequences for actions.
Children are quick studies of adult behavior and character. A well-known
adage says, "It's all about our actions, not our words." I love a saying that I
once heard that applies to my life: *"My parents rarely told me what to do—they
just lived their lives and let me watch!"*

My son, Brad, is CEO and Co-Founder of Freedom Financial Network.
More importantly, he is the father of my two beautiful grandchildren, Brayden
and Brooke. He's been really fortunate (and hard-working) to have been hugely
successful in his work life. One day, he realized that he spent hours of thoughtful time planning and developing his businesses but put much less conscious
thought into his most important resources, his family. So, with his family's
input, he decided to become more systematic in exercising the same efforts
on the home front that he did at work, and the Stroh Family Board Meeting
was conceived. Brad, his wife, Brandy, and their two children began having
monthly family board meetings where, just as in his business, they discussed
what had gone right this past month, what needed a bit of work, and how they
could lead more conscious lives. He developed a form to use as a guideline
for facilitating open discussion and creating a trusting Family Board Meeting
environment.

Now that it is tried and true, he's openly sharing this process with friends, other
family members, and anyone who wants to build more trusting, caring home
environments. The whole process has allowed the parents to be openly vulnerable
and honest and has created an environment of trust where every family member
can bring problems, joyous events, and questions to share with each other.

Stroh Family Board Meeting Agenda

Goal: Ensure that we are living *conscious lives*, where we know the *impact of our actions*, where we *own our paths* through life and take *responsibility for our own happiness.*

Exercises:

1.   What went right or was amazing for me in the past month? _____
_____

2.   Everyone takes turns:
    "I like, I wish, I wonder"
    1.   I like _____
    2.   I wish _____
    3.   I wonder _____
    "Happy, worried, frustrated"
    1.   I am happy about _____
    2.   I am worried about _____
    3.   I am frustrated about _____

3.   Reflection and Planning:
    How we spend our free time:
    •   The things that I spent my free time on in the last month are:
    {are these things we are proud to be a part of, that we are developing with and that make us and/or the world better?}
    Who am I spending my free time with:
    {are these people that we are proud to associate with, that make us and/or the world better?}

4.   What did I do to make the world a better place this month:
_____

5.   My Goals:
    My top three goals for the next month are to:
    1.
    2.
    3.
    {report back on how I did on my goals for the past month}

6.   You Give Me 3 Goals:
    Everyone in the family gives each other a goal to work on over the next month:

1. _____
2. _____
3. _____

{how did I do on the goals you gave me for the past month}

7.   Am I happy? If not, what can I change to make myself happier:
_____

8.   Optional:

    Share a:
    • Poem
    • Picture
    • Book you read
    • Painting
    • Thought or observation
    • Something from nature

9.   Monthly Optional Discussion Topics:
    • Science report about something we are interested in
    • Define our family values
    • Assess our family's impact on our environment
    • Find a service-learning topic that we want to get involved in support-ing, to help less blessed people or things on the planet
    • Read a book together
    • Invite a guest speaker (Auntie Angie & Uncle Joey?)
    • Share a hug

One of my favorite sections of the Board Meeting agenda is where the children are allowed to give the parents feedback on their own behavior. For example, "I know I do some things wrong, but when you tell me about it, I don't learn from yelling and scolding me." Or, "I don't like when you are on the phone or email so much when you are supposed to be playing with me."

The parents might say such things as, "I don't like to have to tell you so many times to do something. Can that be one of your goals for this next month that you do something the first time you are asked or maybe with only one reminder?" Family members set monthly goals for each other and are held accountable to those goals at the next Monthly Board Meeting.

I can't take credit for the genius of Brad's actions, he owns it entirely. The end result and latent discovery is that the process of holding family board meetings shows how much everyone in the family *trusts* each other. In order for the meetings to be successful, every family member has to trust the other enough to know that they can truly say what is on their mind. The children are able to give the parents feedback on the effectiveness of their parenting and the parents are able to discuss the children's problem behaviors in a trusting and safe environment. This Family Board Meeting Mechanic allows for open and frank family discussions. Regardless of your family structure, give it a try. I bet you will find it a useful trust building tool.

Now that we've learned a great deal about building trust in our families, let's examine how we might do this as leaders in our organizations and our workplaces.

NOTES

1.   J. Kiley Hamlin and Karen Wynn, "Young Infants Prefer Prosocial to Antisocial Others," *Cognitive Development*, 26 (1) (2011), 30–39. http://www.cnn.com/video/data/2.0/video/living/2014/02/14/ac-pkg-cooper-baby-lab-part-2.cnn.html.

2.   Walter Mischel, Ebbe B. Ebbesen, and Antonette Raskoff Zeiss, "Cognitive and Attentional Mechanisms in Delay of Gratification," *Journal of Personality and Social Psychology* 21 (1972): 204–218.

3.   Celeste Kidd, Holly Palmeri, and Richard Aslin, "Rational Snacking: Young Children's Decision on the Marshmallow Task Is Moderated by Beliefs about Reliability," *Cognition* 126 (2013): 109–114.

Chapter 12

Leadership and Trust

Followers Who Tell the Truth, and Leaders Who Listen to It, Are an Unbeatable Combination.

—Warren Bennis

THERE IS LITTLE DEBATE THAT employees who trust their employers and like where they work take fewer sick days, have less turnover, and are willing to work harder. They are less likely to sabotage a work environment, bad mouth their employer and the product outside of the workplace, or leave their companies—all things that contribute to the bottom line of any organization.

Robert Levering speaks to this in his recent *100 Best Companies to Work For Study*.[1] When asked to name the one distinguishing factor that separates the 100 Best Companies to Work For from others, Levering claims it's *trust* in the organization and its leadership. Levering has data to back up his claims. He notes that the stock performance of the Fortune 100 Best Companies to work for far outperformed the broader indices—11.8 percent increase for the best companies worked for versus 6.04 percent for the S&P and 6.41 percent for the Russell 3000. These data were tracked over 15 years from 1997–2013.

So, how about you? Think for a moment about the organization for which you work, go to school, or participate in. Do you trust the organization? If you do, why? If you don't, why not? Can the leaders or teachers in these organizations personally do anything to make you trust them or the organization more?

In the next few paragraphs, we will be exploring ways in which leaders can address the issues of trust in the workplace, community organizations, PTA, book clubs, and so on, and build a more trusting environment for their people and their businesses. Hopefully, this chapter will help you decide if you can or cannot trust the leaders in your own workplace, school, or organization, and if you are a leader of a business or organization, hopefully the chapter can help you *become* a more trusted leader.

THE DO'S AND DON'TS
OF TRUSTWORTHY LEADERSHIP

As we've seen throughout this book, building trust is not easy, but if you are leading an organization, regardless of its size, there are behaviors that hold true whether you are building trust with individual employees, supervisors, stockholders, your board of directors, or members of your social organizations. Trusted leaders do a great job with all of the 20 Trust Rules we discussed in Chapters 2 and 3 and those characteristics that represent the Trust Rules Questionnaire in Chapter 9. A few of those items need to be considered more closely.

THE TELLTALE SIGNS OF A TRUSTWORTHY LEADER

Aneil Mishra, Distinguished Professor of Leadership, East Carolina University College of Business, and Karen Aneil, Assistant Professor, Meredith College, claim the ROCC of trust is the key for leaders to build a trusting workplace environment.[2]

The R in ROCC stands for Reliability—having behavior that is stable and consistent. This means being a source of stability in your employees' lives, showing, through your behaviors, that employees can really *rely* on you.

The O in ROCC stands for Openness—the willingness to be honest and direct. While it isn't always possible or wise to divulge all information at all times, it's important for leaders to keep employees truthfully abreast of events that affect their work lives. This openness can show the leader and the corporation as honest and vulnerable, especially when times are challenging. This builds a foundation of trust, so the team never questions the company's motivations or honesty.

On the other side of the equation, trusted business leaders are not afraid to apologize when they've made a mistake. Again, most of us can forgive mistakes. What we can't forgive is the lie when someone pretends the mistake never happened or attempts to cover up for the mistake.

The first C in ROCC stands for Competence. Knowing your job and your business is an essential component of trustworthy leaders. If leaders aren't competent, employees quickly pick up on this. Trustworthy leaders are also truthful when they don't know something. This builds trust. Pretending to have knowledge works the opposite way. As with many things in life, we are able to forgive *not knowing*. What we can't forgive is being untruthful. It's an important reminder that leaders should always tell their employees if they actually know something or if they are just speculating and have an opinion about something. It's an important distinction.

The second C stands for Compassion—being fair and even-handed in sharing information or perspectives. Trusted leaders also attempt to relate to employees on a personal level. They make each individual feel special and a part of the work family. They understand the importance of sincerity. They look out for their employees' best interests, and their employees know it. The know-it-all jerk of a boss who's better than everybody else soon discovers that those employees who can leave for a better work environment, will do so when they are presented the option.

Rhino Foods CEO, Ted Castle, demonstrates this compassion to employees when the business is in a downturn and employees have to be laid off. During these times, he attempts to partner with other local businesses to get temporary employment for those laid-off workers until his business can get back on its feet and he can rehire those employees.

Mishra and Mishra relate another story of Ted Castle, CEO of Rhino Foods, showing compassion for his employees. When Castle overheard a front-line employee noting that his car was out of commission and he couldn't afford to rent another car while his was getting fixed, he threw this employee the keys to the company car and said, "Just return it when your car gets fixed." Employees never forget this level of kindness from their bosses. Now that's what we can call real compassion!

When consulting to organizations and helping them build more trusted leaders, these are the four factors (ROCC) that Mishra and Mishra focus on to enrich trust within an organization. These are clearly important to building trust, but just how do these trusted leaders make it happen?

HOW TO BUILD TRUST IN ORGANIZATIONS

The interviews that I undertook for this book, and the research and consulting I have done throughout my life, have shown me that true trusted leaders have mastered the following three skills. Among others, they are able to:

1. Understand another person's perspective
2. Be an active listener
3. Be an authentic leader

UNDERSTANDING ANOTHER'S PERSPECTIVE—CAN I LEARN IT?

Learning to understand another's perspective is hard work. It takes time and understanding. You have to be open-minded, flexible, and have a constant sense of awareness. You have to be aware that there are most often multiple *right* perspectives, beliefs, ideas, likes, and dislikes. Trusted leaders do their best to view issues from the perception/point of view of the other party.

Perception is how we give meaning to the neurological sensations that our bodies experience. Not unlike an artist who interprets a painting, we also interpret our daily events through a prism of our past experiences.[3] It should not come as a surprise that different people often have different perceptions of the same events. This is a function of our unique histories and different life experiences. No two people will recall an event in exactly the same way. It's not possible.

We have a tendency to view another's actions and reactions through our own lens, or from our perspective, not always digging down to a deeper level of communication to try to understand the other's intentions. It takes a leap beyond that to put ourselves in the other person's shoes and understand what is happening for that person. This is the genesis for misunderstandings that can cripple relationships. Think, for example, of a time when someone misunderstood your intentions or perspective. I bet you found it hard to believe they could have missed the mark so grossly.

Examples of misunderstanding intentions and perspectives are rampant. For example, in the first *Shrek* movie, the star of the movie and ogre, Shrek, overhears a conversation between Princess Fiona and Donkey about "who could ever love something so hideous." Princess Fiona, of course, is talking about herself, as she now turns into an ogre at nightfall and changes back into her former self in the morning. Shrek, however, perceives the comment to be about him and bitterly tells Fiona that he agrees with her, meaning that he understands how no one could ever love *him* as he is the one who is so "hideous." This misperception makes Fiona believe that Shrek won't accept her for the hideous being she has become, and thus, she accepts Lord Farquaad's marriage proposal, instead of building her desired relationship with Shrek. This is one example of how a misunderstanding based on misperception can seriously damage a relationship.

We are all influenced by the way we believe the world works, and we all believe that we have the *real, true, and accurate perspective* about the truth. Yet, because we have a finite amount of energy, sometimes we focus on the unimportant aspects of events and miss the relevant issue. To avoid this problem we must learn to develop ways to become better at perceiving and understanding others' perceptions.

Our different perceptions of an issue or event can unwittingly engender conflict. When one person sees x and another person sees y and neither is willing to accept that the other person's perception is valid, conflict ensues. We attribute *our* meanings to actions and behaviors but these may not be real for the other person. We often judge ourselves by our intentions and others by their actions.[4] It is the meaning of an action, however, that is important to holding conflict at bay and essential to formulating plans to resolve conflict. Differences in personal perspectives are often at the core of conflict in organizations.

When we can understand the other person's perspective, we build trust. When getting real with perspectives, we begin to realize that:

- we sometimes don't see what is there
- we may overlook important aspects of a conversation/interaction

- we see what we want to see
- there are often multiple *right* perspectives
- it's easy to fool us in the direction *we* want to go and EASY to convince ourselves that our reality is the only *right* reality

Being sensitive to another's perspective IS trust building. You've undoubtedly heard many times, "We don't always remember what you have to say to us, but we ALWAYS remember how you made us feel." When we accept that there are often multiple correct perspectives, we have taken an important step forward in trust building.

BEING A GOOD LISTENER

Given that we do a lot of listening, you would think we would be pretty good at it. We've all had a lot of experience with listening, but experts tell us that most of us only hear anywhere from 25–50 percent of our communication with other people.[5] How do you feel knowing that your boss, colleague, spouse/ partner, or friend only hears 25 percent of what you say?

Experts tell us that good listening skills help us become more effective and efficient in our workplace relationships and help us build trusting relationships (this is true in our personal lives, as well!). So, another way for leaders to build trust in their organizations is to be good listeners. Good listeners show concern for others, are open, and are respectful. I like to say that they understand that listening isn't a passive sport.

One way to become a good listener is to embrace *active* listening. Active listening is a communication technique that requires the listener to repeat what he or she has heard as confirmation of listening and understanding. We will be exploring the techniques of probing, paraphrasing, and nonverbal cues in more detail and give some suggestions for becoming a more active listener. With active listening, we attempt to *really* hear what people are saying. Experts say that active listeners are more trusted and more effective in the workplace and in relationships in general. No doubt we can all benefit from learning how to become better communicators. This skill can also help us determine if our leaders can be trusted.

BECOMING AN ACTIVE LISTENER

Richard Branson, CEO and founder of Virgin Airlines, frequently cites listening as one of the main factors behind the success of Virgin Airlines. Effective listening is a skill that underpins all positive human relationships. Spend some time thinking about and developing your listening skills, for they are the building blocks of success. As Mark Twain said: "*If we were supposed to talk more than we listen, we would have two tongues and one ear.*"

James Manktelow, CEO of MindTools, and his colleague Amy Carlson claim there are five key elements of active listening.

- Pay attention. Pay attention not only to what someone is saying to you, but also pay attention to the nonverbal cues that person may be displaying. Does that person appear uncomfortable, at ease, anxious, or happy? Try to look directly at the speaker to avoid being distracted by other events happening in your environment. Don't think about how you will respond to what this person is saying, just listen. Give your undivided attention. While listening isn't a passive sport, it's not a competitive sport either. Don't be strategizing the next point you want to make in this exchange.

- Show that you are listening. Show that you are listening to the speaker by using your own body language. Use your own facial expressions to let the speaker know you are paying attention by nodding, smiling, or frowning.

- Provide feedback. Provide feedback by repeating what the other person has said, asking clarifying questions, and/or summarizing what you have heard.

- Defer judgment. Defer judgment by not interrupting with *counter arguments*, even though it's tempting to do so.

- Respond appropriately. Active listening or not interrupting the speaker doesn't mean that you agree with what that person has said. When the speaker has finished, respond respectfully, be honest, and offer your own thoughts in a respectful way.

It's no secret that most of us have some pretty bad listening skills and it will take time to break these bad habits. It takes practice. Again, I like to say that listening is not a passive sport! Keep practicing at getting better at listening, just as you would practice to get better at your golf game, your tennis game, or playing the piano.

Robert Shafir, author of *The Zen of Listening*, claims another good way to think about becoming a better listener is to try to get into other peoples' *movie*. [6] He uses the term *movie* to describe other peoples' lives—who they are, what their story is.

Shafir says that, by listening to someone else as if we were watching a movie, we aren't *pretending* to listen or *working* at listening, we are instead *really* listening to the other person. When we are watching a movie, we aren't thinking about what we are going to say next, about how our life relates to this person, or what we want to interrupt and say. Instead, we are totally listening to the person who is speaking. We *enter into his or her situation.*

Shafir claims that this movie mindset also creates a situation where we are much less willing to interrupt someone. He claims that the more we practice the movie mindset of listening, the better we get at it and the more we will notice how people respond positively to our natural, attentive listening. When we listen with a movie mindset, we immerse ourselves in the perspective of other people. While we may still disagree with what other people may have said, we are now less judgmental in our disagreement because we more fully understand another person's point of view.

The movie mindset makes even more sense when we realize we often get so involved in a movie that we can truly feel the actors' emotions, often shedding a tear or relating fully with the emotions on the screen. Doesn't it make sense to incorporate this movie mindset into our listening repertoire?

Shafir notes that to be a good listener we have to get out of our own *movie* and self-concerns and into the movie of our conversant. The best part about Shafir's listening strategy is that there are no steps to learn, no mantras to remember, because the movie mindset should just be an extension of our own curiosity.

So, after your next conversation, evaluate yourself on the following active listening skills:

- Making eye contact
- Paraphrasing
- Avoiding interruptions
- Avoiding distractions
- Not overtalking
- Asking clarifying questions
- Getting into the other person's movie

Once we master the ability to take different perspectives and learn to listen actively, we are well on our way to becoming an authentic leader.

AUTHENTIC LEADERSHIP AND TRUST BUILDING

People trust authentic and genuine leaders, but what do those terms mean and what qualities does an authentic leader possess? Can we learn them or are they innate qualities? Bill George, Professor of Management at Harvard Business School, and his colleagues say, yes, we can learn to be authentic leaders.[7] For these researchers, the key is to know yourself and understand that it is a gift to serve and lead others.

Most people associate authentic leadership with *who* you are, not *what* you do. In describing an authentic leader, some characteristics that come to mind are genuineness, courage, and a profound sense of self-awareness. It's a long-term commitment to self-development. Authentic leaders remember their past. They remember where they have been.

"Most authentic leaders have highly developed social antennae: They use a complex mix of cognitive and observational skills to recognize what followers are consciously—and unconsciously—signaling to them."[8] Their words are consistent with their actions, and they are able to relate to people on their own terms and from their perspectives.

Authentic leaders understand the true meaning of success. Success is often not measured by a bank account, address, or job title, but rather by honesty, self-awareness, flexibility, and the ability to be *real*. Sue Desmond-Hellmann, the Gates Foundation CEO (the world's largest charitable organization) claims that authentic leaders show up as themselves everyday.[9]

So what does all this mean and how do we learn it? Margie Warrell posits that authentic people allow themselves to be vulnerable and connect with others from a "place of being human a bit better than the rest of us."[10] They are individuals who, while they care about whether others like them or not, do not change themselves to be better liked. They understand themselves and like the uniqueness of the persons they are. Authentic leaders aren't afraid to give negative feedback to others but do so in thoughtful ways.

Authentic leaders think of themselves as servants to their employees and constituents. They are often more interested in the contributions they can make over time rather than the short-term goals of today. Dr. Hardwin Mead, world-renowned cardiologist and recipient of the 2015 Cardiac Care Excellence Award, is one such leader and states that people believe us to be trustworthy leaders when we can act justly, love mercifully, and walk humbly.

Authentic leaders know themselves, are self-aware, and consider their lives a lifelong research study to learn about themselves and how to develop over time into healthier and healthier adults. They also have *relentless mental discipline*.[11] They develop a healthy mental script and maintain a discipline over it.

As I often say, our lives are full of imperfection. We just have to determine what level of imperfection we are willing to live with. Our goal, then, is to become our very best *imperfect* selves!

So, can *one* individual influence trust in an organization through her/his actions? The answer is yes. The means to this end include:

- Constantly reinforcing values of reliability, openness, compassion, and competence
- Being totally transparent at all times. If compromise is necessary, never sacrifice your core values
- Remembering that it is a privilege to be a leader, not an entitlement
- Having the ability to listen to and seek different opinions and perspectives
- Being able to handle conflict effectively
- Showing up as your real self every day

Doing these simple things over time *earns* trust. Give it a try!

Now, let's take a look at how the Internet and the digital age have affected our trust decisions.

NOTES

1.   CBS *Sunday Morning*, August 31, 2014.

2.   Aneil Mishra and Karen Mishra, *Becoming a Trustworthy Leader* (East Sussex: Routledge, 2013).

3.   Linda K. Stroh, Gregory Northcraft, and Margaret Neale, *Organizational Behavior: A Management Challenge* (Mahwah, New Jersey: Lawrence Erlbaum Associates, Publishers, 2002).

4.   http://www.huffingtonpost.com/peter-fuda/change-efforts-fail-becau_b _6498442.html.

5.   James Manktelow and Amy Carlson, *Active Listening: Hear What People Are Really Saying*; http://www.mindtools.com/CommSkll/ActiveListening.html.

6.   Rebecca Z. Shafir, *The Zen of Listening* (Wheaton: Quest Books, 2000).

7.   Bill George, Peter Sims, Andrew McLean, and Diana Mayer, "Discovering Your Authentic Leadership," *Harvard Business Review* (February, 2007).

8.   Robert Goffee and Gareth Jones, "Managing Authenticity: The Paradox of Great Leadership." *Harvard Business Review* (December 1, 2005).

9.   Bill Snyder, "Gates Foundation CEO: Good Intentions Aren't Enough," *Insights by Stanford* (January 23, 2015)

10.   Margie Warrell, "Why Leaders Must 'Get Real'—5 Ways to Unlock Authentic Leadership," *Forbes* (May 20, 2013).

11.   Ibid.

Chapter 13

Trust in the Digital Age

The Thing about Quotes on the Internet is You Cannot Confirm Their Validity.

—Abraham Lincoln[1]

WE HUMANS HAVE USED TRUST as a survival tool since the beginning of time. And the methods for determining if someone is trustworthy have been pretty consistent throughout our history: appearance, verbal and nonverbal communication, reputations, and family. And while there are many different ways for individuals to establish trust, the common denominator has always been the *in person* interaction. It has only been recently, with modern technological advances, that assessing trust has become much more convoluted. The bogus Internet quote above is a perfect example of this complexity. Of course, while Abraham Lincoln knew nothing of quotes on the Internet (or the Internet either, for that matter), there is no doubt that we have come to a critical trust juncture as the Internet continues to evolve.

Over the past 30 years, technology has transformed both the world and our lives. More than any other piece of modern technology, the creature we call the Internet has revolutionized the way in which we interact with one another and has impacted the way in which we assess and establish trust. For most of us, learning whom we can and cannot trust on the Internet has been somewhat trial and error. Where we used to have conversations in person, we now use cell phones to call or text. Where we used to share life events over lunch and dinner dates, we often now use Facebook and other social media to announce life changes to "friends," some of whom we may have never met in person. Where we used to go out into the world in search of companions, love, or marriage, many of us now stay at home and use online websites such as eHarmony and Match.com to find possible love interests. It seems that life can now be reduced to a few simple clicks on a website.

ADVANTAGES OF THE INTERNET

There is no denying the many positive benefits of technology and the Internet. We have instant access to an exuberant amount of information regarding any and every topic ranging from geography to history to math to biology. We can connect with people from all over the world. We can telecommute in our jobs, never even leaving our homes. The Internet has opened up new labor and commercial markets. In fact, the list of the Internet's benefits could fill up this entire book. Nearly every aspect of our lives has been enhanced by technological advances. In our schools, our workplaces, our homes, and our friendships, there is no doubt the Internet has allowed us to learn more, learn it faster, and learn it more handily. And, unlike earlier forms of technology, the use of the Internet is rarely exclusive. Most in our country have easy access to the Internet, regardless of location, age, gender, race, or other demographics. For most of us, access to free Wi-Fi is fairly easily available, in our schools, in our coffee shops, even in our grocery stores. All of this can be pretty exciting and wonderful! But . . . is there a downside?

THE INTERNET CHANGES OUR SENSE OF TRUST

Most everything comes with a cost. And the cost of this modern technology is no exception, especially in regards to its impact on trust. While use of the Internet allows us to connect and learn more and learn it faster, it simultaneously has the potential of becoming our own personal, local, national or international downfall, because even with the Internet, *trust* remains the cornerstone of a well-functioning society at the interpersonal, local, state, national, and even international levels. A breakdown of trust at any of these levels is devastating to varying degrees.

Still, people have become habituated to reveal every detail of their intimate lives without realizing the potential threats or consequences of their full disclosure. Social media sites such as Facebook, Twitter, Instagram, and Snapchat have given people the opportunity to share their lives with each other. Unfortunately, however, anything we put on the Internet is there *forever*. Let me repeat this sentiment: *Every e-mail, picture, story, blog, location, and thought that we put on the Internet will never go away. EVER!* And still, people don't think twice about sharing their family vacation photos on Shutterfly or ranting about their crazy boss on Facebook. These forms of social media can cause us immense problems, when we assume the information is being sent to someone in private or will not be viewed by specific people.

Take the case of former congressman Andrew Weiner, who was involved in two scandals related to sexting, the sending of explicit sexual material by cell phone. Do you think Weiner ever imagined his photos would hit the front page news? Of course not. Do you think he mistakenly trusted the person to whom he was sexting these materials? Of course he did. His misplaced Internet trust cost him his career, his seat in Congress, and a lot of personal pain, heartache, and humiliation for himself and his family.

WE SHOULD THINK BEFORE WE POST

When we are considering a new job, we should be aware that potential future employers are checking social media sites to gain better information about the candidates applying for positions at their firms. That picture of us trashed in Cabo during spring break may be funny to our friends, but it does little to leave a positive impression on our potential future boss. So, from a trust perspective, remember that anything we place online can be saved forever, and can be forwarded to anyone with a computer, be it the chancellor at our school, our dean, our adviser, our clients, our boss, or the president of our company. Worse yet—our moms! Even if we aren't motivated to *do the right thing* because it's the *right thing to do*, do it regardless, as a matter of self-preservation. We should think before we post or text, because what we *do* post can be used against us at any time in our lives—FOREVER. We should all just pretend that we're sending out every message to the entire world every time we go online. Everyone is listening, everyone is watching.

Keep in mind also that not everyone who shares personal information *with* us can be trusted. The term catfishing was coined to describe the phenomenon of Internet predators who fabricate online identities and entire social circles to trick people into emotional/romantic relationships (over a long period of time). There is an entire show on MTV called Catfish, dedicated to this form of distrust. The show helps people who are emotionally entangled with someone they have met over the Internet but have never met in real life. Each episode is an investigation into whether or not the other participant in the virtual relationship is legitimate or, in fact, a "catfish." Some couples have been communicating for a few months, others for years and, more often than not, the individual has been found to be lying about his or her identity.

THERE'S MORE . . .

The Internet has also given rise to new forms of bullying we would have never expected to have to deal with. One of my favorite sayings is, "It's difficult to 'hate' up close," yet the Internet provides a barrier between us and others that allows us to "hate" in new and harmful ways. Cyber bullying can take many forms, including sending mean threats via email or cell phones, spreading harmful rumors online, or posting hurtful or threatening messages on social media sites. Teenage suicides due to Internet bullying, while continuing to sadden us, no longer shock us! In fact, according to bullyingstatistics.org, as of 2015, over half of adolescents and teens have been cyber bullied, and there have been over 41 suicides due to cyber bullying since 2003. This is a devastating statistic that demonstrates the very real consequences that can occur when we side-step the face-to-face requirement for establishing and developing trust and the problems that can result when the buffer zone of the Internet filters out this humanity.

The consequences for individuals are not limited to social media. The Internet has changed our lives in so many ways. E-commerce, which refers to any business-to-consumer transactions, such as online retail or online auctions, has become a huge part of today's society and not only includes transactions between individuals but also trust between individuals and companies.

Craigslist is a classic example of a website where fraud can occur and trust is sometimes broken. Many individuals freely give their personal information and enter into financial transactions without first reliably establishing trust. If the provider of the goods is untrustworthy, the transaction becomes a one-way affair. The individual pays for a product that is never delivered. We can avoid this pitfall by becoming aware and educating ourselves. Nearly every retail store now has a website where we can order their merchandise online. Individuals can now bank online, sell their furniture online, file their taxes online, and even apply for college online. If we have business to conduct, we're most likely going to be conducting it online. The possibilities are abundant and endless, but there is risk. We'll have to enter personal information, such as our address, phone numbers, and credit card information. Unfortunately, divulging this personal information online can have negative consequences. In March 2011, California-based insurer HealthNet announced a privacy breach for nearly 2 million of its customers, exposing their names, addresses, Social Security numbers, health, and financial data—bummer!

BIG BROTHER

Trust issues are not simply limited to information we personally enter onto a website. Search engines such as Google and Yahoo also gather information about our searches, with or without our knowledge. In fact, one of the biggest scandals broke in 2013 when it was leaked that the government was collecting information about U.S. citizens. Yahoo, Microsoft, Facebook, and Google were all found to have been providing the NSA with U.S. citizens' personal information. Whom Can You Trust Online? It's a tough question without an easy answer.

The success of the Internet or any Internet website depends on its ability to earn the trust of its users, and just as in our pre-Internet days, trust continues to be at the center of successful business dealings. eBay's founder, Pierre Omidyar, could not have said it better: "Our business depends on people conducting transactions, and people don't conduct transactions unless they have a trusting relationship first." That is why companies, such as Google, are attempting to gain back their customers' trust. Google has recently been working on bringing an improved version of PGP (Pretty Good Privacy) to encrypt emails on the client side. This means that no one, not even Google, can look at an email except for the sender and the receiver of that e-mail. Time will tell if these changes will help Google build back its customers' trust.

TRUST ON THE INTERNATIONAL SCENE

The recent Sony company hack is an excellent example of the ways in which breaches of trust can occur at an international level. In 2014, hackers infiltrated the computer network of Sony Pictures Entertainment, a major Hollywood movie studio. The attackers stole and leaked a number of confidential documents, including top employees' salaries, nasty Hollywood hardball e-mails, and illicit movie downloads. It has been speculated that the hack was instigated by North Korea, upset at Sony for producing *The Interview*, a movie that depicts the assassination of North Korean leader Kim Jong Un. Again, this is a prime example of the ways in which information that we may think is secure on the Internet can later be used against us when trust is breached.

So, with all this in mind, how do we even begin to assess trust on the Internet?

WHOM *CAN* WE TRUST ON THE INTERNET?

Well, there is good news. We can be proactive in our own search for trust on the Internet. Just as in our personal relationships, we can never be 100 percent sure if a website is perfectly trustworthy, but we can learn some of the signs that make it more probable that we can safely use a website, download an APP, or post on Facebook. Here are a few tips to remember:

1. Use secure and trustworthy Wi-Fi.

2. Keep security software up to date.

3. Avoid paying for hotspots.

4. A web site that uses HTTPS in the address bar is the most trustworthy. Without HTTPS in the address bar, we should never give out personal data.

5. A lock in the address bar suggests it is more difficult for a hacker to gain the information that you type.

6. Only shop at sites that have the Better Business Bureaus online website seal of approval (be careful here, however, as some sites can just copy these seals and paste on their sites, so this isn't always a guarantee).

7. Never open a link in an e-mail from someone we do not know. This is one of the sure-fire gimmicks for those trying to gain access to our personal data.

8. Use safe programs such as PayPal when dealing with private individuals or companies we are unfamiliar with.

9. Watch for misspellings and simple grammatical errors that indicate the site may be a foreign hack job.

10. Remember that the government will never send you an e-mail requesting information. They use snail mail.

SUMMARY

With changing technology, crimes are changing too, making it easier to commit fraud, impersonation, and theft and more difficult for us to know whom we can and can't trust. Crime is now being committed from a distance, and governments, laws, and policies aren't able to keep up with the fast-paced discovery of new Internet technologies. It is all changing so rapidly that we are often struggling to stay abreast of the changes. The pace will continue and new technologies will, no doubt, bring us many rewards. But we have to continue to question at what costs do we enjoy these new technologies? While we gain amazing access, we lose many privacy rights. Governments, businesses, friends, and even our enemies have access to much of our most private information and personal experiences. While the Internet has forced us to consider trust in many different ways, the truth still remains that *trust* continues to be the foundation of our relationships and interactions, whether face to face or on the Internet.

Well, now, we've learned a lot about how we can tell the difference between good guys and bad guys, how to build more trusting families and workplaces, and how to deal in trusting ways on the Internet. Regardless, sometimes we are still stuck living or working with people we know we can't trust. The next chapter will help us figure out how to do a better job of that!

NOTE

1.   This is an anonymous quote taken from Pinterest.

Chapter 14

Living and Working with Untrustworthy People

Conflict is inevitable, but combat is optional.

—Max Lucade

SOMETIMES DOING THE GOOD guy/bad guy calculation leads us to the awareness that we are often forced to live, work, or share our lives in some way with people we do not really trust. These aren't people that just aren't trustworthy enough to be part of our inner circle, or those people with whom we have conditional trust relationships. These are people the Trust Rules Questionnaire has revealed to be totally untrustworthy and may be colleagues, neighbors, friends of friends, or even family. What do we do when we are forced into this situation, sometimes not by our own choice, but by someone else's? Would/should our behavior and decisions vary, depending on whether we are dealing with an untrustworthy person in our work or personal lives? How do we handle these trust dilemmas? The story below may be a helpful starting point.

SOMETIMES AMBITION CAN OVERRIDE GOOD JUDGMENT

I left a good job to work for a company that was in serious financial trouble. I was offered a minority ownership of the company as additional compensation when I joined. Despite the apparent problems, I did not do personal reference checks or do any research beyond my own questioning of them. I was impressed with the opportunity to "run my own company." I took, at face value, the representations made to me by the owners of this privately held company. I was naïve and gullible. Ultimately it became apparent that the two owners lacked character and integrity—they proved to be dishonest and were not to be trusted—had I been more reflective and discerning of them I would probably have reached this conclusion earlier. In order to disentangle myself from this work relationship, I had to set down criteria as to what they had to do to make restitution and to redress their wrongs.

I put into place an oversight plan so I didn't ever need to trust them again.

I was able to successfully turn the company around and protect my friends and former work associates and customers. I was fortunate, as it certainly could have turned out otherwise. The moral of the story is not to take things at face value, do your due diligence, step back from situations, and reflect before committing. I let my ambition get the best of me. I vowed to never make that mistake again.

—Samuel Browner, Chairman, President, and CEO, Tortuous, Inc.[1]

Browner's experience shows that, when forced to work, live, or otherwise share our lives in some way with someone who is untrustworthy, we must first never forget with whom we are dealing, and we must put significant controls in place so that we are not harmed by their untrustworthy behaviors. If we do a good job with the Trust Rules Toolkit, and we appropriately assess a bad guy's untrustworthiness, we'll know what we are up against and can remain on top of the situation. We may have to place boundaries around when/where/how we will work with these untrustworthy people.

HOW DO WE BUILD THOSE BOUNDARIES?

Successful people, both at work and in their personal lives, employ a specific behavioral protocol when forced to work and/or live with people they don't trust. The old adage, a *good offense is the best defense*, comes to mind. Here's what those I interviewed for this study recommend.

First, to be a good guy yourself, be absolutely certain that the person is, in fact, untrustworthy. You must distinguish between your *suspicion* that a person is untrustworthy and has a potential to harm and actual *evidence* that the person is untrustworthy and harmful.

Second, be extremely cautious about what you say while the untrustworthy person is listening, so your words cannot be misconstrued or used out of context. Limit your interactions with this person as much as possible.

Third, as a last resort, after the person has demonstrated consistent untrustworthiness, mobilize your allies; speak to them in advance of any important meetings/and or conversations to discuss how you will manage the untrustworthy person. Be constantly ready for battle, yet never begin a confrontation. Remember, being prepared doesn't mean you are going into a conversation/meeting with this person with your cannons loaded, but rather that you are prepared for what is a predictable, negative interaction with someone you know is untrustworthy. Mobilizing your allies should be a last-resort effort.

Fourth, prepare! Before entering conversations/meetings with the untrustworthy person, decide beforehand what he or she might want—and make sure you have prepared counterarguments. If you and this *untrustworthy* person's goals are aligned, it's likely that he/she will be more trustworthy. Listen to what the person has to say before responding with a counterargument. Your foe just might be making a rational, logical comment (not probable, but possible).

Fifth, do much more listening than speaking around the untrustworthy person. Take great pains to listen, and when the untrustworthy person refers to something you have said, be prepared to correct him or her immediately, in a nonconfrontational way. For example, "John, that is not what I said. What I said was . . ." Often, you may head off this situation by never discussing any personal beliefs or history and being cautious never to reveal what you thought of someone, what you expect to happen in some instance, or any personal background.

Sixth, limit as much as possible your interactions with the untrustworthy person to situations that constrain or eliminate discretionary behaviors. As Dr. Faye Crosby noted:

NEUTRALIZE THE BAD GUYS

I try to figure out the ways a bad guy might be harmful to me and neutralize him or her along those dimensions. I try to contain the toxicity, isolating the bad guy; segmenting the toxicity; or just getting away from it as much as possible. For example, I did get a divorce and I do live 3,000 miles from people who would otherwise continue to cause me pain.

—Dr. Faye Crosby, Provost, Cowell College and
Professor of Psychology, University of California
Santa Cruz

Dr. Crosby recommends that we manage our interactions with bad guys as much as possible. If we aren't confident we can deal with any *bad* the untrustworthy person can create, she suggests we must protect ourselves mentally, physically, and spiritually by removing the person from our lives to the greatest extent possible.

Seventh, never forget that a negative interaction can be one in which the untrustworthy person is contentious and difficult to get along with, but it is equally as likely to be one in which the untrustworthy person is using charisma and charm to win you over. In fact, the latter is probably the most dangerous situation of all, in that the unaware and trusting person can be easily duped. Be prepared for the charm, as well as for the confrontation.

Eighth, while this might be impossible in our personal lives, it is of vital importance in the workplace to be as transparent as possible. Document every important decision/conversation in writing, both what you say to the untrustworthy person and what the untrustworthy person says to you. Doing so eliminates the chance you will be misquoted and provides a written, evidential record. There will be times when you may find it prudent, for your own protection, to forward this documentation to people in authority.

Name-dropping is another tool you might consider using with the untrustworthy colleague/friend/family member. For example, instead of getting into a verbal sparring match about some issue, mention you've already discussed the issue with the VP or CEO (mom/dad/sister/president of the homeowners association) and they really liked it!

Dealing with bad guys does seem a bit dicey, doesn't it? The important common denominator here, however, is that whatever we do, we do without malicious intent. If we cross that border into *bad guy* activities, we can drag ourselves down to the lowest common denominator and can become bad guys, like our untrustworthy foes.

BE VIGILANT

After structure comes vigilance. Vigilance is an awareness that not everyone is worthy of our trust. Being vigilant means we should exercise caution in our interactions with those we have identified as untrustworthy. In these instances, we should validate any important information we receive from the untrustworthy person and never take at face value any important information the untrustworthy individual may provide.

To end this chapter, here's a story about working with bad guys that reminds us of the importance of having the confidence to make those tough *bad-guy* calls. This story shows how easily it is to continue to fool ourselves about good guys and bad guys and how we often want to even pretend they are something they are not.

BUT SHE IS A THIEF

Your question about figuring out how to live/work with bad guys reminds me of the story of a secretary who was caught using the company's purchasing credit card for personal items (which in itself is not a crime), but then having the company pay the bill. The auditors eventually caught her and she was fired. She was clearly mortified, as if that matters. Some weeks later, her supervisor came to see me and said that she had called, asking for a reference. I told him that he should not provide a reference; that he should tell her all employment verifications are handled by the call center and he could not otherwise comment as a matter of policy.

He looks at me and says, "But she doesn't want anyone to think she is a thief!" And I said, "But, she is!"

—Nicole Friedman, Senior VP Human Resources,
The Camden Corporation[2]

To sum up, when working or living with untrustworthy people:

- Establish with absolute *certainty* the person is untrustworthy.
- Be cautious of what you say around the untrustworthy person; limit your interactions with the untrustworthy person.
- Mobilize your resources; avoid confrontation at all costs.
- Be prepared!
- Listen more; talk less.
- Head 'em off at the pass. You know what they are likely to say to your boss, colleague, neighbor, mother, relative—so present your different/more accurate viewpoint early and often.
- Limit interactions to *strong situations*, in which cultural norms limit discretionary behaviors.
- Be especially careful of the charmer, yet recognize times when your goals may be aligned.
- Be transparent. Document as much as possible.
- NEVER forget with whom you are dealing.
- Be vigilant.
- Do whatever you do without malicious intent.

Next, let's consider "Why Do Those Bad Guys Do That Bad Stuff?"

NOTES

1. The names of this person and the company have been changed to preserve anonymity.
2. The names of this person and the company have been changed to preserve anonymity.

Chapter 15

Shattered Trust: Why Do Those Bad Guys Do That Bad Stuff?

Forgive your enemies, but never forget their names.

—John F. Kennedy

A FTER WE'VE SITUATED OUR CURRENT and potential confidants in their appropriate spots on the trust continuum, we soon discover that all of our relationships have imperfections, even the best ones. We next have to decide what level of imperfection we are willing to live with. In prior chapters our focus was on learning what constitutes trust and assessing the level of trustworthiness in others. In this chapter, we'll look at why some people betray others. Having a better understanding of why some people do bad things, and whether they will do those bad things again, may help us decide whether we should repair or relinquish a shattered relationship.

STUNNED AND SPEECHLESS

When we are close enough to someone to consider that person a confidant, we can blow off the little stuff—those snippy criticisms of something we did—and chalk it up to someone having a bad day. We can tolerate quite a bit from our dearest confidants. That's not what this chapter is about. This chapter is about the stop-you-dead-in-your-tracks errors of judgment or behaviors, the ones that leave us stunned and speechless and make us wonder if we can ever speak to that person again. Let's begin this chapter, then, with an analysis of what goes wrong and ask why some people consciously or unconsciously harm others.

WHAT IN THE WORLD WENT WRONG

Those explosions that shatter trust among friends are often tied to violations of deeply held values or beliefs, such as dignity, honor, or pride. They make us question just what went wrong. These shared values are what created the inner circle to begin with, so when these values are fractured, the relationship is bound to crumble. The biggest rifts are personal. They harm us emotionally. Sometimes they're intentional, but other times we're merely dealing with another's immaturity or thoughtlessness. We should be mindful of this distinction as we decide what to do.

One of my most interesting conversations about trust and betrayal was with Dr. Thomas Dicke, MD, a nationally recognized physician/specialist from the Midwest. Dr. Dicke is one of those sage doctors that friends, neighbors, and people of all ages turn to when they need advice. I met with Dr. Dicke in Hawaii. Over coffee, with a warm ocean breeze blowing, Dr. Dicke shared his thoughts as to how and why people engage in bad behaviors. Dicke's comments are among the most succinct and profound I encountered. Dicke claims it isn't easy to tell the good guys from the bad guys and notes it's easy to be wrong, because people can be hard to read, especially those with little integrity and those who think nothing of lying.

BAD GUYS BELIEVE THEMSELVES

Some people become so good at telling lies that they begin to believe the lies themselves. That makes it even more difficult to tell the good guys from the bad guys, because they become so good at lying. It becomes second nature to them.

Good people are honest, they're good communicators, and they are willing to be transparent. Bad people have difficulty with honesty. It's really like a sickness in some ways—egos have a lot to do with it. So I like to ask myself, "Does this person think of themselves first, or others?" And I ask myself, "Are they even capable of thinking of others, instead of just themselves?"

BAD GUYS HAVE UNDERDEVELOPED EGOS

Dicke reminded me that it's important to remember everyone has different levels of ego development. Selfish people, or some bad guys, have underdeveloped egos. There are complex theories that explain bad-guy behaviors, but Dr. Dicke had a nutshell way of describing them. He says that one reason people do bad things is that their egos let them down: They are angry and they then lash out at something or someone. He noted that we all have defense mechanisms to protect our egos. Some people have psychologically healthy defense mechanisms; he calls these people *good guys* and *trustworthy*. Others have defense mechanisms that are psychologically unhealthy; those Dr. Dicke calls *bad guys* and *untrustworthy*. He presented the following synopsis:

BAD GUYS NEED A BETTER HOBBY

Say, for example, someone starts feeling a bit down because they've lost at something, as we all do; a game, work, a relationship, etc.

Those with healthy egos have defense mechanisms that help protect their egos in ways that are psychologically and socially healthy. It's an important part of successful development that we do.

For example, they might read a book, do some woodwork (like I do), take a walk, work out, play tennis, or some other socially acceptable ways to protect their egos when things go wrong for them. Others with unhealthy egos might do something less socially acceptable. For example, if they lost their job, they might rob a bank to get more money for their family. They might also cheat, lie, or do something else to try to build up their ego and avoid dealing with the real issue: the job loss, or whatever went wrong in the first place. Others might have affairs and build their egos by having someone flatter them in that way. The point is someone with a weak ego will do almost anything to make themselves feel better and avoid dealing with the real issue inside of them. For these people there are no limits to how far they will go to get what they want to make themselves feel better and thereby keep their ego intact. So, some have socially acceptable ways of dealing with their disappointments and controversies in their lives; others do not.

Bad guys lash out at someone or something else when things go wrong in their own lives. The mature person (ego) would use diversion instead to distract the mind/body/spirit to regain a state of equilibrium and a better perspective, a healthy, ego-protective activity. Those who do not have the cognitive and emotional skills to determine a better alternative when they are feeling badly will do something *bad* to make themselves feel better (lash out at someone, have an affair, rob a bank, drink, eat too many cookies), which usually, in the longer term, makes them feel even worse. You will remember that we discussed some of this in the earlier chapter about emotions and trust.

The second reason people behave badly, Dicke says, is that they aren't able to delay gratification; they lack the willpower to be good. Those who are more cognitively and emotionally mature are able to put off their negative feelings until they regain a sense of equilibrium, allowing them to behave in more productive and socially acceptable ways. An important point here is that the emotion is not buried or repressed or forgotten. Instead, the individual becomes self-reflective and is later able to view the difficult situation in more objective terms.

I DIDN'T MEAN TO DO IT

Those with immature egos are often unaware they are being selfish. They label their actions in ways that make what they've done seem okay to them. They might claim that circumstances or some person caused them to behave in this or that way. So, according to Dr. Dicke, to develop a healthy ego, we have to be willing to objectively reflect on our behavior and assess our level of selfishness to see how our behavior affects others, not just ourselves.

Let's examine some of these *bad-guy* behaviors. As Professor Black notes, one of the worst bad-guy behaviors is selfishness.

ME! IT'S ALL ABOUT ME!

Like most people, I get a gut instinct about whether someone is good or bad pretty quickly. I pay attention to this first impression, but do not just go with it. Judging truly bad people is easy. What's hard is identifying people who are not good. For this I rely on the two criteria my grandmother stressed when I was a young boy: selfishness and deceit. In her view, if someone is selfish and not honest to boot, steer clear. They're likely to help themselves and hurt you, then try to hide this until it's too late.

—J. Stewart Black, Professor of Leadership and Organizational Behavior, INSEAD, and President, Global Leadership Institute

Learning to become unselfish, to mature, grow, and become better people with healthy ego adaptations requires us to bring the *unconscious* to a *conscious* level. Bad guys can't do this. Part of our unconscious ego system is always trying to get us to behave badly—to bring out our bad side. Dr. Dicke said:

IT TAKES STRENGTH TO ADMIT TO WEAKNESSES

I've found it's most often the person who thinks they don't have any insecurities who is the most insecure of all and the most dangerous type of people to have as a confidant. These people are afraid to admit to any weakness or that anything is wrong in their life, which is the biggest weakness of all. They continue to cover up their insecurities in ways that don't allow them to grow in positive ways; cheat more, or lie more to protect their egos, rather than admit that something is wrong in their life. Until bad guys are willing to admit to being human and having weaknesses, they often continue in a spiral of behavior that is harmful to themselves and others.

But, no matter how mature we are, sometimes our ego lets us down. We do something selfish or that may feel good for a while. We all do it, but those with healthy egos then feel a sense of guilt and are filled with remorse and want to make it right with others. They admit their mistakes and say they are sorry for their mistakes. Here's where the really bad people get into trouble; they don't feel enough remorse for doing bad things that are harmful to others and then just continue in that vein. They won't let themselves think how they are hurting other people by lying, cheating, or being selfish, and they often never learn to become better people, because they spend so much time covering up their insecurities in negative ways.

Joseph Tripodi, Chief Marketing and Commercial Officer, The Coca-Cola Co., calls this the inflated ego syndrome (IES). Tripodi tells us that bad guys' egos rarely let them consider the well-being of others. They are unable to manage their egos and, thus, can do great harm to others, usually with little awareness of, or concern for, the harm they've done. We read earlier that we can get along with someone who has IES when our goals are aligned with theirs. The problem is, when our goals are unaligned, we can be assured a problem will occur. The trick is not to be seduced by the charisma of a big ego and to be aware that a goal-aligned link is temporary and tentative at best. Here's what Tripodi has to say about IES and its relationship to good guys and bad guys:

SORRY? SORRY FOR WHAT?

A major defining element of good guys versus bad guys, in both work and personal life, is the capacity to control one's ego. I have personally witnessed so many individuals who get so consumed by their own hubris that it completely blinds them to reality and truth. We all have egos; it really is a question of how we manage our egos. When I look at all the recent corporate scandals, it is clear to me that inflated egos and subsequent greed drove individuals to do things that were way out of the bounds of normal behavior. What inflates these egos to the point that they should be floats in the Macy's Thanksgiving Day Parade? Who knows? Personal insecurity? A mindless celebrity culture that grossly exaggerates the contributions of individuals?

In a fairly short period of time, one can diagnose if someone suffers from IES—inflated ego syndrome. When I see IES, it is a clear signal to be cautious.

—Joseph V. Tripodi, Chief Marketing and
Commercial Officer, The Coca-Cola Co.

New York State Supreme Court Justice Joseph McGuire notes there is a term called "Robe-itis" that refers to judges whose egos have run amok. He noted that when he became a justice, all of a sudden his jokes were funnier, he was more handsome, his clothes, hair, and person just seemed to look better to others. There is no doubt that with success and power, for those with weak egos, there is a chance for their egos to get out of control. Now add others' intentions to want to be near important, successful people and the result may not be pretty. To prevent an out-of-control ego, Justice McGuire cautions that, as good guys, we must insist that people be honest and real with us and challenge us to be honest and real, too. The result will then be a more trustworthy relationship.

I DIDN'T DO ANYTHING WRONG

Dicke's final comments emphasized that bad guys may betray us because they simply don't think about their behavior in objective ways. They spend their time trying to convince themselves and others they didn't make a mistake. Then they cover up their weaknesses, which results in even more mistakes, rather than spending their time learning what they did wrong and how to change their behaviors. According to Dicke, unless these people learn from their mistakes, the likelihood they will harm us again is quite high. From Dicke's conversation, we can see that we should carefully consider these aspects when we are deciding about second chances.

Dr. Dicke stressed that he is the first to admit his generalizations are simplistic, and more detailed explanations exist regarding why someone may behave badly. But, for me, Dr. Dicke's explanation is profound in its simplicity.

SUMMARY

In this chapter, we've discussed some reasons why bad guys behave badly. We've also learned some strategies for protecting ourselves when we're forced to interact with them.

We've all been around people with little ability to empathize with the situations or feelings of others. Developmental psychologists would tell us that being able to empathize is a complex set of both cognitive and emotional skills, allowing us to understand how our behaviors affect others. In order to be able to take another's perspective, we must have the cognitive and emotional ability to actually place ourselves in that person's situation and view the world from that individual's perspective.

We enter this world with egocentric perspectives. Then, hopefully, as we mature, we begin to see the personal benefits of helping others so they will help us. This stage is instrumental in that we want something in return for being helpful to another. If we get really lucky and evolve more fully, we begin to understand the universality of *good* and understand the importance of generalizing our behaviors universally. That is, we are able to ask ourselves the question, "*What kind of a world would this be, if everyone did what I just did? If everyone lied, cheated, or was dishonest in some way?*" Or, more positively, "*What kind of world would this be, if everyone were unselfish, forgiving, thoughtful, and kind?*"

To be successful in our own work and personal lives, we must understand why *bad guys* do *bad things* and make decisions about whether we are willing to give someone a second chance. Read on . . .

Chapter 16

What about a Second Chance?

Forgiveness is the economy of the heart . . . Forgiveness saves the expense of anger, the cost of hatred, the waste of spirits.

—Hannah More

EVEN REALLY GOOD GUYS sometimes make mistakes. Thus, part of the good guy/bad guy assessment involves deciding whether we should give someone a second chance when that person has betrayed our trust in some way. To better understand when that second chance is worth it, it's important to understand what factors might influence our willingness to consider giving a trusted confidant a second chance. Here, we'll consider the influences of religion, culture, the media/pop culture, and also what the scholarly research has to say about forgiveness and reconciliation.

RELIGION

The concept of forgiveness is often written about and discussed within the context of religion. Most religions encourage us to forgive, on the belief that forgiveness is noble. Our religious beliefs might persuade us to forgive, but are there times when this is the wrong action to take? Let's consider some of the world's major religions and their teachings on the subject.

Christianity

In the Christian tradition, one of the most widely read and discussed examples of forgiveness is the parable of the Prodigal Son. As the story goes, a man decided that, upon his death, his property was to be divided equally between his two sons. The younger son didn't want to wait to enjoy his inheritance and his father's wealth. Thus, he asked his father for his share immediately. The father agreed and the younger son moved far from his family and squandered his fortune on wild living. A famine ensued and the son was forced to live a destitute existence, rummaging for food and work. One day, the younger son decided to return to his father in hopes of working in his father's fields, knowing that his father's workers had a better life than he did. The father welcomed the younger son back with open arms, even killing a fattened calf to celebrate the event.

What's the moral of this story? It's part of the Christian ethos that we forgive those who ask for forgiveness. We have a spiritual obligation to do so. The Bible teaches that a fundamental element of Christianity is God's forgiveness of our original sin. God forgives us for our transgressions and, likewise, expects us to forgive others. This forgiveness expectation is grounded in every aspect of the Christian tradition. We find it in the Lord's Prayer: ". . . forgive us our debts as we forgive our debtors." The Christian religion reminds us often of our responsibility to forgive when others harm us.

Judaism

Yom Kippur, the holiest of days for Jews, is the Day of Repentance. Just as Jews are required to ask forgiveness of God and of all people they have harmed, they are also required to forgive others. A prayer recited on this day includes these lines: "I extend complete forgiveness to everyone who has sinned against me, whether physically or monetarily, or spoken lashon hara (negative speech) about me or even false reports . . . And just as I forgive everyone, so should You grant me favor in the eyes of all men, that they should completely forgive me."

As with Christianity, a fundamental tenet of Judaism is forgiveness.

Buddhism

The Buddhist parable about two monks walking on a muddy road may also have important implications for how we think about forgiveness and reconciliation. The story goes something like this:

Two monks were walking in the rain along a muddy road. They came around a bend to a river they had to cross to get to their final destination. At the river they found a beautiful woman dressed inappropriately for crossing the river. The first monk said to the woman, "Come with us. I will help you cross the river." He then lifted the woman into his arms and carried her across the river and placed her back on solid ground.

Neither monk spoke until later that night when they finally reached their temple. The second monk could wait no longer and said to the first monk, "You know we monks are not supposed to go near females and especially never touch them. We know this is a very dangerous thing for us to do."

The first monk replied, "Yes, but I left the woman at the river's bank. Why do you still carry her?"

The second monk clearly could not forgive the first monk for doing what he perceived as something wrong. Thus, the second monk continued to carry the misdeed with him. What can we take away from this Buddhist parable? *Forgive or you can't move on with your life.* You keep carrying the emotional baggage around with you in your mind. Buddhists forgive in order to prevent negative emotions that affect a peaceful mental well-being. Negative feelings, feelings of resentment, retribution, and the like, create a mindset of ill-will that prevents the cultivation of a peaceful existence with life in general, and in our minds, in particular.

Hinduism

A Hindu parable shows how our willingness to forgive may be more tied to the person we are than to another's act of betrayal. In this lesson, a notable lord was intentionally testing his kings, asking a particularly evil and selfish one of them to travel the world to find one truly good man. This evil king met and conversed with many in the lands and, after years had passed, returned to the lord and reported that he had searched the whole world and could not find even one really good man. This evil king noted that all men were selfish and bad.

The lord then asked another very kindly king to find a really wicked person. This kindly king also traveled all over the world and returned to the lord and reported that he could not find any truly evil men. The king noted that there were men who had made mistakes, were foolish, ill-advised, but that most men were good-hearted. This lord clearly forgave each person for their transgressions, rather than harboring hate and resentment toward those who did wrong.

The moral of this Hindu parable is that our general perceptions of human beings affect the way we respond to an act of betrayal. If our inclinations are to be kind and naturally forgiving, we are more likely to be kind and forgiving and see kindness and forgiveness in others. Conversely, if our inclinations are to be evil and unforgiving, we are more likely to be evil and unforgiving and be more likely to see evil in others, as well.

Another basic premise of Hinduism is that forgiving others is a measure of strength. Those unable to forgive rob themselves of supreme peace; those who are able to forgive are powerful. A Hindu prayer emphasizes the importance of forgiving and being forgiven:

> O Lord, forgive three sins that are due to my human limitations:
> Thou art everywhere, but I worship you here;
> Thou art without form, but I worship you in these forms;
> Thou needest no praise, yet I offer you these prayers and salutations,
> Lord, forgive three sins that are due to my human limitations.

Once again, we see the influence of religious beliefs on our willingness to forgive and that understanding our humanness is the first step toward forgiveness.

Islam

In Islam, Allah commands His followers to forgive those who do them wrong. One Islamic story concerns a prophet commanded by Allah to forgive those who did harm to him. This prophet was often treated miserably when preaching the messages of Allah. Nevertheless, he prayed that Allah would forgive them because they acted out of ignorance.

Those who have read the Koran are aware that Islamic teaching makes it clear that it is always better to forgive those who betray us. Given that we base our human existence on Allah's forgiveness of our sins, we too must forgive the wrongdoings of others. Allah rewards those who pardon others with His forgiveness as well.

The concept of forgiveness is a thread common to all religions. Although we may not all be able to embrace the concept of forgiveness in our lives, our religious teachings have exposed us to the concept that forgiveness has a moral basis, and it is our obligation to forgive.

CULTURE

While we are often aware of the influence that religion places on our willingness to forgive, we sometimes overlook the ways in which cultural and historical norms speak to us about the concept of forgiveness. Most people would agree that our culture has a huge influence on the people we become. Many times it's not the clothes we wear, the art, food, ceremonies, and other trappings we can see that impact us the most. It's the invisible aspects of culture (the myths, stories, verbal histories) that may have the most power. These subliminal messages influence how we think and feel about forgiveness.

In a previous book, I used a tree as a metaphor for understanding culture and its influences on our lives. The branches and leaves, the visible components, are the tangible parts of our culture—what we can see, hear, smell, taste, or touch. My coauthors and I referred to these aspects of our culture as *artifacts*. These artifacts are the manifestations of the roots or the more underlying values and assumptions shared by people of similar cultures. Passed from generation to generation, these roots serve as mental roadmaps, guiding many of our observable behaviors. The more deeply they're held, the more influence they have on who we are and how we behave.[1]

Therefore, questions concerning the nature of human relationships can be culturally grounded. What is the right way for people to deal with each other? How much power and authority should one person have over another? To better understand behaviors, we must first understand the invisible values and assumptions that we hold and the stories we carry with us. These stories are carried forward as archetypes in our literature.

LITERATURE

Dante's *Divine Comedy* is a literary example often used as an illustration of what happens when someone, unwilling to forgive, continues to seek revenge. In this epic poem, former political allies Count Ugolino della Gherardesca and the Archbishop Ruggieri degli Ubaldini become bitter rivals. Ultimately, Ugolino is betrayed and murdered by Ruggieri.

They bear such hatred for each other that even death cannot end their enmity. Their souls are consigned to hell, and Dante later finds them frozen together in the same hole, the Count gnawing on the Archbishop's skull, consumed with eternal hunger for vengeance. The application to our own lives is easy enough to understand. Revenge and bitterness work to harm the victim even more than the victimizer and place the victim and the victimizer in a hell of eternal revenge.

We next look to Shakespeare to continue our literary examination of the theme of forgiveness. In *The Winter's Tale*, written in 1623, an outwardly perfect family is ruined by an unwillingness to forgive. While the play ends with a reconciliation of the king, queen, and their long-lost daughter, there is much intervening anguish and pain suffered by all, because the king believes his wife has been unfaithful and he is unwilling to forgive her.

In the example of Dante's *Divine Comedy*, the combatants lost the opportunity window of forgiveness and were consigned to eternal punishment. In *The Winter's Tale* example, forgiveness (reconciliation) takes place before the end of Act V. This reconciliation frees the characters from their self-inflicted purgatory on earth. The lesson in this literature is clear: Those who cannot forgive do not themselves receive forgiveness.

MEDIA/POP CULTURE

While we can debate whether the media and pop culture create the messages or merely reflect where a society has already gone, it's clear that the media and pop culture at least perpetuate the sense that for good guys, to forgive is divine. Forgiveness and revenge as themes run through a recent list of Academy Award-nominated films:

- *Frozen* (Relationships cannot be rebuilt without forgiveness, such as between Elsa and Ana);
- *Maleficent* (The power of betrayal and forgiveness between Maleficent and Aurora);
- *The Hobbit* (Strong aspects of forgiveness throughout all the movies, both between individuals and groups);
- *The Theory of Everything* (The betrayal and forgiveness between a husband and wife);
- *12 Years a Slave* (Asks for forgiveness from family and attempts forgiveness of slave owners).

There are at least two messages perpetuated in pop culture. The first message is about the bad guys. Bad guys do not give second chances and, when wronged, they seek revenge. For example, in *The Godfather*, the bad guys never forgive and forget. In this powerful story about transgression and betrayal, Michael Corleone had his brother, Fredo, killed for his acts of betrayal. The same was true for his brother-in-law, Carlo Rizzi. The code of the bad guys: "Don't give someone a second chance, even your blood relatives. You'll pay the price if you do." Revenge and betrayal have become big themes in pop culture.

There is even a TV show called *Revenge* on ABC, whose plot follows a young woman as she takes revenge on those who betrayed her father. The TV show depicts just how long-lasting the emotion of revenge can be and how far-reaching it is. The basic message coming from these pop-culture references is that when wronged, we should seek revenge and not forgiveness or reconciliation.

Alternatively, a more powerful message in the popular media might be that good guys do forgive others, and they also ask for forgiveness themselves. *My Name Is Earl*, the Emmy award-winning television sitcom, gained popularity at all socio-economic levels. While some may find it impossible to draw parallels among Shakespeare, Dante, and Earl, important cultural influences nevertheless do exist.

In this sitcom, Earl develops a list of those he has transgressed in some way. He has experienced an epiphany in his life and wants to ask forgiveness from those he has wronged. Earl is initially motivated by karma, defined by Earl as a force that will eventually punish him if he does not make right what he has done wrong in his life. However, as the story unfolds and Earl is given redemption by some of those on his list, he begins to discover feelings he had not previously recognized. While Earl's intentions early on were self-serving (to avoid punishment through karma), he comes to realize that he has seriously harmed people. Now operating unselfishly, he begins to right the wrongs. Earl demonstrates a life lesson: If we are good guys and allow ourselves to be reflective about our behaviors, we will know when we have done harm and will want to rectify those wrongs. This TV show is now aging, and, it's interesting to note that no new show that explores the benefits of forgiveness for both the betrayer and the betrayed seems to have taken its place. Does this say anything about media/pop culture and the interests of our society? Or just about the short-sightedness of producers and top TV moguls?

On a more serious note, the award-winning movie, *The Color Purple* (first a classic novel and later a sold-out Broadway play), provides another example of how the victim suffers, if unwilling to forgive. Because she wanted to sing secular music, Shug Avery became estranged from her father. After decades of extensive travel as a jazz singer, there is a powerful scene where Shug begins singing her own well-known song in a local bar near her father's church. The sounds of her voice drift into the church during her father's sermon. The church choir begins to sing, "God Might Be Trying to Tell You Something." Hearing the song, Shug leaves the bar. She, too, begins singing the choir's song as she walks to her father's church, enters the door, approaches her father and embraces him in an act of forgiveness and reconciliation. Her father, in a return gesture of forgiveness, accepts the embrace.

Once again, these pop culture examples represent a similar, basic tenet of our religious and cultural lives: If we're good guys and we forgive and forget, we can live better lives. We are clearly surrounded by forces encouraging us to forgive, from religious parables and both visible and invisible aspects of our culture. But does that mean forgiving is always the right thing to do—in every situation?

SCHOLARLY RESEARCH

It is only recently that academics have begun to study the nature of forgiveness. Forgiveness doesn't mean you now trust someone who has betrayed you or that you are willing to reconcile. It merely means you are letting go of your anger and resentment.

Kathleen Lawler and associates, researchers from the University of Tennessee, claim that forgiveness has unique benefits to your health. The benefits include improved sleep quality and reduced fatigue. One of the strongest findings in their study, however, was the reduction in negative affect (feelings of tension, anger, or depression).[2] Similarly, Hannon and associates found that when an individual who had been betrayed forgave the betrayer, both experienced a decrease in blood pressure.[3] And recently, Toussaint and colleagues found that developing a more forgiving coping style when dealing with betrayal may help minimize stress-related disorders.[4] From this handful of research studies, it is clear that forgiveness can have considerable physical and mental benefits to the forgiver. Other research shows the relationship also benefits.

While negative events or conflict can sometimes threaten otherwise positive relationships, Driver and associates explain that the real test of a relationship's strength is how the relationship reacts to conflicts related to a breach of trust. These researchers claim we can learn a great deal about the concept of trust as we examine how/when, or if we should repair a trusted relationship.[5] Likewise, research by Renate Ysseldyk and Michael Wohl shows that forgiveness can promote a stronger commitment to a relationship after a relationship has endured a severe offense.[6]

Another recent study from Ashley Heintzelman and associates, researchers from the University of Missouri-Kansas City, found that couples that experience infidelity were able to save their relationship when the partner who was wronged truly forgave the other. In fact, the relationship actually became stronger when true forgiveness occurred, achieving what the researchers termed Post Traumatic Growth (PTG).[7] Therefore, even in the face of infidelity and betrayal, couples *can* recover and even become stronger when forgiveness is achieved. Kim, Dirks, Cooper, and Ferrin profess that a relationship is most likely to be repaired when the betrayer is willing to bear some additional negative elements to continue with the friendship.[8] We will discuss some of these elements later in this chapter.

Interestingly, the benefits of forgiveness hold true for not only the couple, but also for other family members involved. Kristina Koop Gordon and her colleagues found that forgiveness of a marital betrayal is positively associated not only with marital satisfaction, but also with the parenting alliance and children's perception of parental marital functioning.[9]

However, forgiveness is not just a one-way street, according to Pelucchi, Paleari, Regalia, and Fincham who have also studied the effects of forgiveness on relationships. These researchers have focused on self-forgiveness, forgiving oneself after committing some type of betrayal. They claim that self-forgiveness is not only related to personal well-being, but also contributes to greater relationship satisfaction. Here, the notion is that in order for relationships to fully recover after acts of betrayal, forgiveness must not only come externally, but also internally.[10]

Focusing specifically on the workplace, Cox, Bennet, Tripp, and Aquino found that those who forgave their coworkers for moral reasons (because they felt it was the right thing to do) reported less stress and greater health than those who believed they had no other choice than to forgive.[11]

Pratt and Dirks argue that the most positive relationships are grounded in trust, yet must be resilient and generative. They note that most trusting relationships have inevitable episodes of challenge and times of both personal growth and tests of relational toughness. They use the metaphor of a broken bone to point to the importance of properly repairing a valued relationship. If we have a broken bone and the break is set properly, the bone may be stronger than ever and allow the person to live life as fully and completely as before the break. However, if the bone is improperly repaired, it will cause ongoing pain and suffering. Metaphorically, these authors claim when trust is broken in a relationship and is properly reset, the relationship can be stronger than ever and continue to thrive, but if the relationship is not repaired properly, both parties can suffer for a long, long time.[12]

Reconciliation is dependent on both parties' willingness to renew a relationship, but the probability of the reconciliation being successful is greater when the betrayer firsts asks for forgiveness. This allows the betrayed person to feel more in control with the choice to then rebuild the relationship, or at least decide whether to forgive the betrayer. For Pratt and Dirks, restoring a balance between the positives and negatives in a relationship is the important part of restoring a broken relationship.

Pratt and Dirks agree that relationships tested by betrayal and then successfully restored may be even stronger than untested relationships. The lengthy process of reconciliation binds together both positive and negative aspects of strong relationships. Thus, both parties in the relationship, having been through difficult times together, know they have the necessary skill-set to apply to any future conflicts.

SUMMARY

After reviewing the ways that religion, culture, media/pop culture, and scholarly research influence our willingness to give someone a second chance, a few conclusions become clear. The overwhelming evidence is that good guys should forgive those who betray them, but bad guys just can't!

Good guys are able to recognize that those with healthy self-esteem do not betray others. Thus, they realize that forgiveness is about forgiving someone for their cognitive, emotional, or physical weaknesses.

If forgiveness is such a good thing and we are bombarded with messages telling us it is better to forgive than not, then why are there so many shattered relationships where we are unable to forgive? Keep reading . . .

NOTES

1.   Linda K. Stroh, J. Stewart Black, Mark E. Mendenhall, and Hal B. Gregersen, *International Assignments: An Integration of Strategy, Research, and Practice* (New Jersey: Lawrence Erlbaum Associates, 2005).

2.   Kathleen A. Lawler, Jarred W. Younger, Rachel L. Piferi, Rebecca L. Jobe, Kimberly A. Edmondson, and Warren H. Jones, "The Unique Effects of Forgiveness on Health: An Exploration of Pathways." *Journal of Behavioral Medicine* 28(2) (2005): 157–67.

3.   Peggy A. Hannon, Eli J. Finkel, Madoka Kumashiro, and Caryle E. Rusbult, "The Soothing Effects of Forgiveness on Victims' Perpetrators' Blood Pressure." *Personal Relationships*, 19: (2012): 279–289.

4.   Lauren Toussaint, Grant Shields, Gabriel Dorn, and George M. Slavich, "Effects of Lifetime Stress Exposure on Mental and Physical Health in Young Adulthood: How Stress Degrades and Forgiveness Protects Health." *Journal of Health Psychology*. August: (2014).

5.   J. Driver, A. Tabares, A. Shapiro, E.Y. Nahm, and J. Gottman, "Interactional Patterns in Marital Success or Failure: Gottman Laboratory Studies," in *Normal Family Process: Growing Diversity and Complexity*, ed. F. Walsh, 493–513 (New York: Guilford, 2003).

6.   Renate Ysseldyk and Michael J. A. Wohl, "I Forgive Therefore I'm Committed: A Longitudinal Examination of Commitment after a Romantic Relationship Transgression." *Journal of Behavioural Science/Revue* 44(4), (2012): 257–263.

7.   Ashley Heintzelman, Nancy L. Murdock, Romana C. Krycak, and Larissa Seay, "Recovery From Infidelity: Differentiation of Self, Trauma, Forgiveness, and Posttraumatic Growth Among Couples in Continuing Relationships." *Couple and Family Psychology: Research and Practice*, Vol 3(1), (2014), 13–29.

8.   Peter Kim, Donald L. Ferrin, Cecily Cooper, and Kurt T. Dirks, "Removing the Shadow of Suspicion: The Effects of Apology vs. Denial for Repairing Competence vs. Integrity-based Trust Violations," *Journal of Applied Psychology* 89 (2004): 104–18.

9.   Kristina Coop Gordon, Farrah M. Hughes, Nathan D. Tomcik, Lee J. Dixon, and Samantha C. Litzinger, "Widening Spheres of Impact: The Role of Forgiveness in Marital and Family Functioning." *Journal of Family Psychology*, 23(1), (2009), 1–13.

10.   Sara Pelucchi, Giorgia F. Paleari, Camillo Regalia, and Frank D. Fincham, "Self-Forgiveness in Romantic Relationships: It Matters to Both of Us." *Journal of Family Psychology*, 27(4), (2013): 541–549.

11.   Susie S. Cox, Rebecca J. Bennett, Thomas M. Tripp, and Karl Aquino, "An Empirical Test of Forgiveness Motives' Effects on Employees' Health and Well-being." *Journal of Occupational Health Psychology*, 17(3), (2012): 330–340.

12.   Michael Pratt and Kurt Dirks, "Rebuilding Trust and Restoring Positive Relationships: A Commitment-Based View of Trust," in *Exploring Positive Relationships at Work*, ed. Jane E. Dutton and Belle Rose Ragins, 117–36 (New Jersey: Lawrence Erlbaum Associates, 2007).

Chapter 17

What Is Forgiveness?

The weak can never forgive. Forgiveness is the attribute of the strong.

—Mahatma Gandhi

W E'VE DISCUSSED TRUSTWORTHINESS and its evil twin, untrustworthiness, and their relationship to how we live and work with good and bad guys. We've also spent some time situating the climate of forgiveness within our culture. Now we'll consider *our* relationship to forgiveness: doling it out or holding it back. What follows is a short exercise that should prove fruitful for you.

First, think of a friend or colleague, spouse/partner, someone you trust and would feel comfortable soliciting feedback from. Now, imagine this person has betrayed you in some way. Under what conditions would you be willing to forgive this person? What is it about that relationship that is valuable to you? Take a moment to think about this scenario.

Now, imagine a negative relationship, someone you never really trusted or someone who has hurt you in some irreparable way. What is different about these two relationships? The answer will lead you to an understanding of the conditions under which you would be willing to forgive. Before you read on, take a moment to reflect on both of those conditions.

Forgiveness is the psychological or spiritual ability to let go of resentment and anger toward another person. I read somewhere that forgiveness is not an action, but a discovery. In this psychological state, we are willing to quit punishing someone for acts that we perceive as harmful to us in some way. The two scenarios at the beginning of this chapter attest to the fact that the act of forgiveness is a choice. Most psychological theory would point to the healthy spiritual and mental aspects of forgiveness. There are also reported physical health benefits related to one's capacity to forgive another. As we think about good guys and bad guys in our lives, it's important to understand how the concept of forgiveness plays into building, developing, and maintaining healthy relationships with those good guys with whom we work and live.

IT'S OUR CHOICE

At some point, we will undoubtedly find ourselves in situations in which the person who victimized us is unable or unwilling to say a simple *sorry*. In these instances, it is important to remember that forgiving someone is *our* choice, not that of the person who has harmed us. It is well documented that hanging on to anger harms the betrayed more than the betrayer. This adage says it all: *Hating people is like burning down your own house to get rid of a rat.*

Forgiveness is easier when the transgressor asks for forgiveness, but a victim can choose to forgive even if the wrongdoer never asks. In 2006, a gunman killed six girls at a school in the Amish community. He then turned the gun on himself. There was no apology—the gunman was dead—but the families, acting in accordance with their religious beliefs, chose to forgive him.

Forgiving does not mean forgetting. It also doesn't mean we have to continue to have this person be a part of our lives. Forgiving simply means we have let go of resentment and anger. In fact, forgiving means we have acknowledged the pain/hurt/disappointment but have made an active *choice* to discontinue punishing the person who was disloyal to us. In contrast, forgetting means we do not remember the betrayal and haven't learned from it, which may set us up for yet another disappointment.

One interviewee for this book illustrated this concept with a quote from her mother: "You forgive and forget, but you always remember." The logic is a little convoluted, but it means you have to put the incident out of the foreground or you can't move on. So in that sense, it is a kind of *forgetting*. Still, you need to keep the betrayal close enough to be a reminder should you find yourself going down that same wrong road again.

So, is forgiveness always good? I would posit: Yes, it is, because it allows us to rid ourselves of the angst. What we don't have to do, however, is let someone back into our lives as a trusted friend or confidant.

As Rick Lenny responded, when I asked him if he ever gives someone a second chance:

I Don't Hold Grudges

Oh, yeah—if I forgive myself, I have to forgive others. I don't hold grudges. I can't. It is very difficult for me to hold grudges. The person who holds a grudge is the one who suffers. The person to whom the grudge is directed has probably already moved on and they don't even think about the problem any longer.

—Richard H. Lenny, Former Chairman of the Board, President and CEO, Hershey Company

Most of us would agree, however, that for forgiveness to be the most effective for the victim, the transgressor must be sincerely remorseful for the undesirable behavior, atone for that behavior, and ask forgiveness. We've watched way too many politicians, athletes, and business leaders who have been coached by their consultants to publicly apologize for a wrong. Most make feeble attempts and fall far short of convincing us they were really sorry, suggesting rather that they were merely sorry they were caught.

STILL REBUFFED

Martha Stewart is still rebuffed by some, because she never fully admitted to a mistake she made with her financial consultants and her access to insider information in personal stock trades. Many believe that had she done so early in the investigation, she might never have spent a day in jail. Many of those who live their lives in the public eye and then falter spend more time on a cover-up than they did in the harmful act. Stewart is no exception.

Lance Armstrong and his now well-known doping scandal also comes to mind. Armstrong's reputation was shattered after he publicly admitted to doping to win the Tour de France a whopping seven times. Although he had consistently denied allegations of doping for months, he finally confessed during a broadcast interview with Oprah Winfrey. Armstrong made a public apology during the Oprah interview. "I view this situation as one big lie I repeated a lot of times," he said. "I made those decisions, they were my mistake and I'm here to say sorry."[1]

Armstrong would have gained our respect more had he initially acknowledged the mistake of doping instead of denying the allegations for so long. Once again, we see that the greatest fall from grace does not come from the initial poor choice in behavior, but rather from the constant lying and denying any wrongdoing occurred. As it was, Armstrong's apology seemed somewhat hollow.

Our apologies have to show an awareness of the harm that was done, not just that we feel guilty or sorry; otherwise, the apology appears to be one given because the guilty parties were caught making a mistake and not because they sincerely recognize they did harm to other people.

Armstrong's apology would have been more credible had he immediately acknowledged the mistake of doping and given up his marathon trophy to the runner-up. Stewart could have been forgiven in the public forum had she shown she understood that when those who have access to greater information about stock trades take advantage of the system, the rest of us participating in that market pay the price.

These examples illustrate that it is always best to admit mistakes, examine why we made them, show we understand the harm we have done, and ask for forgiveness. Most people accept that we aren't perfect but don't accept or forgive us when we don't assume responsibility for the mistakes we do make. This is especially true when we continue to try to fool others and ourselves by engaging in cover-ups that try to prove our innocence. Interestingly, while most public people are forgiven for even egregious acts of betrayal, attempting a cover-up almost always turns the public away for good.

SOME DO IT RIGHT

Some in the public eye do, however, do it right. In 2007, JetBlue, an airline company, had a week-long operations collapse after an ice storm hit the East Coast of the United States. Most other airline companies had cancelled their flights early, sending passengers home, and resumed their schedules days later. JetBlue, however, didn't want to cancel flights preemptively, thinking that the weather might break. They thought this would keep its revenue flowing and its customers happy; however, this plan backfired. The company ended up with over 1,000 cancelled flights in just 5 days. Even more tragically, one airplane full of angry passengers sat for six hours or more stranded on the tarmac at JFK international airport. And although the company could have blamed external factors, such as the weather, for this disaster, the CEO of JetBlue, David Neeleman, took responsibility for the problem, arguing that this event was a result of the poor management and communications system within the company.

He wrote a public letter of apology to the 131,000 JetBlue customers affected by this event. He introduced a Customer's Bill of Rights, which offered explicit compensation for a variety of departure delays and onboard ground delays. He also went on YouTube, the Today Show, Letterman, and Anderson Cooper, not to play the blame game, but just to apologize for his company's faults. Neeleman was also quoted as saying, "This is going to be a different company because of this. It's going to be expensive. But what's more important is to win back people's confidence."[2]

Although there was still some backlash and much of the company's reputation was damaged, Neeleman did everything he could to restore the reputation of JetBlue and take responsibility for the event.

Johnson & Johnson and the Tylenol recall in 1982 come quickly to mind as yet another example of *doing forgiveness right*. James E. Burke was Chairman of the Board of Johnson & Johnson at the time of the national crisis, in which seven people died as a result of a packaging design of the Extra Strength Tylenol™ capsule that allowed someone to add 65 milligrams of cyanide to some capsules—far more than a lethal dose. Rather than push the blame on a distributor, a seller, or someone else, Burke quickly made the decision to remove all product from shelves and counters and recall all Extra Strength Tylenol™ products, thereby taking responsibility for the problem. In addition, Burke offered to replace any Tylenol™ capsule with product from a competitor.

Johnson & Johnson developed a new, more secure cap. As a result of what has been called the best public relations story in our history, we feel safe using the Tylenol™ product. Burke and Johnson & Johnson did everything right to preserve the reputation of the company. When asked how he knew this was the right thing to do, Burke stated it was an easy decision. He noted that the company followed the credo established by Robert Wood Johnson in the 1940s. That credo claimed Johnson & Johnson was in existence to be responsible to society, not just to the company. This credo led Burke and Johnson & Johnson to do the right thing for both them and their consumers.

The Johnson & Johnson story is a shining example of how, when asking for forgiveness is done right, reconciliation can occur and create an even stronger relationship than before. Johnson & Johnson willingly and immediately admitted to a mistake, rather than engage in a lengthy cover-up. They demonstrated their trustworthiness to their consumers, and the consumers *bought* it. Again, most of us accept that people aren't perfect. What we don't accept is arrogance!

Choosing to forgive is the moral high ground. It's elevating. Choosing to forgive may lower your blood pressure, lengthen your life, and even create new opportunities for growth. Forgive your enemies. You'll be a better person for it. You may also teach them an important lesson, if they're open to it. But even if they're not, forgive them anyway. Just don't forget!

NOTES

1.   http://www.oprah.com/own/Lance-Armstrong-Confesses-to-Oprah-Video
2.   http://www.nytimes.com/2007/02/19/business/19jetblue.html?pagewanted=al

Chapter 18

Reconciliation

If we could read the secret history of our enemies, we should find in each person's life sorrow and suffering enough to disarm all hostility.

—Henry Wadsworth Longfellow

OK. SO WE'VE ANALYZED AND considered the value of our relationships, both with those we trust and with those we don't. We've been betrayed, let down, or disappointed and have decided to forgive. What's next?

While forgiveness is an important part of healing after a serious betrayal, the much tougher decision is about reconciliation, giving someone a second chance at trust. Many egregious acts of betrayal create such ugliness that reconciliation is nearly impossible, but there are some situations where even a serious betrayal can work to develop a more trusting relationship than ever before. This more trusting relationship may be between individuals, or in the Johnson & Johnson example, between a company and its customers.

Let's now imagine we've been wronged in some way. We've already determined the betrayal is extremely serious, something that violated the core of the relationship. How do we decide where to go next? My research has shown that most of us are more willing to reconcile with someone if we can adequately:

1. Assess the seriousness of the betrayal

2. Understand why the act(s) were done

3. Decide whether we can live with the personal ramifications of the betrayal

4. Decide whether we can live with the impact of the betrayal on others

5. Determine if the betrayer understands the harm caused and is truly sorry for what was done

6. Assess if the betrayer has learned from the mistake and will not harm us again

Negotiating each of these stages takes time, reflection, and soul-searching. In the next section, we'll examine each of these steps in depth, use them to analyze a betrayal in our lives, and determine if reconciliation is warranted.

STEP 1: ANALYZE THE BREACH OF TRUST

As we analyze a breach of trust, we must ask ourselves some serious questions. How serious or significant is the problem? Does the breach of trust affect our core values? Are there some wrongs that we will never forgive because they affect us at our deepest level? How public was the betrayal?

We also must assess whether this was a single enormous betrayal or a series of small errors. While the former is obviously harmful, a series of small betrayals can be equally as devastating to a relationship. Small betrayals might be acts of omission, just *forgetting* to tell the boss you showed the report to the competitor; or hinting that a project was nearly completed, when it hadn't even been started; or forgetting to tell your spouse/partner that you received a phone call from an old girlfriend/boyfriend; or not mentioning you had spent too much money this month on unnecessary items; or being impatient, overly critical, and/or unkind in conversation.

As these small deceptions accumulate, they can create circumstances equally as devastating as a betrayal that is wider in scope in that seeds of doubt and untrustworthiness are planted and begin to filter into the relationship. While these minor betrayals may be unintentional, their outcome can be just as serious as a huge mistake, as they work to undermine and chip away at the essential features of a trusted relationship.[1]

Did the betrayal occur at work or in our personal lives? While most people agree that we are less likely to give someone a second chance in our work lives and more likely to do so in our personal lives, this is something we must consider: Does it make a difference?

For Rick Lenny, *truth* is a core value and he has no tolerance for those who are not truthful:

I CALL IT LYING

> Some people call lying being disingenuous. I call it lying. I just won't tolerate lying. I have a job to do and deciding not to tolerate lying is an easy part of that job. In personal situations, that's a tougher challenge. I'd be much more lenient, but I would know that I have to be careful about what type of relationship I will have with them. It would be a relationship-altering perspective.
>
> —Richard H. Lenny, Former Chairman of the Board,
> President, and CEO, Hershey Company

Another important issue when considering reconciliation with someone who has betrayed us is the embarrassment and/or humiliation of the betrayal. We all know that humiliation of any form is difficult to accept, but public humiliation is the most difficult of all and often forces us to be less willing to forgive.

One of my interviewees recalled:

BULLY SYSTEM OF CONTROL

I remember an incident during a teacher in-service, where the principal berated someone who had confided in him. The principal dragged out every detail of the confidential conversation in a very public way. He had allied himself with a faction that was focused on disrupting morale. Sort of the "bully system" of control. He went public and ballistic. It was a terrible situation.

—Jonathan Lynch, Teacher, Southwest Public High School[2]

It's important to fully understand the reconciliation process, in order to successfully resolve troubled relationships. As noted earlier in this chapter, if you've decided the problem falls into the category of a friendly disagreement, you may choose to have a conversation with your confidant about it and quickly rectify the problem. If, however, the answers to these questions make you realize that the breach is truly significant and one not easily ignored, proceed to Step 2 and each subsequent step. This will ensure you do not make your decision about reconciliation too quickly. Those who move through the reconciliation stages hastily are more likely to have a subsequent problem with this betrayer or with others later on.

STEP 2: UNDERSTANDING WHY THE PERSON WRONGED YOU

Understanding why someone betrayed us is the next step. This will allow us to assess whether we will take the time and emotional energy to repair the relationship. In other words, to what do we attribute the mistakes that were made? What meaning do we assign to the act of betrayal? Were the negative behaviors a permanent/stable part of the person's behavior, or were the behaviors out of character for this person? The intentions we attach to the behaviors have important implications for how we will react in the future toward this person.

At this stage of the assessment process we must determine what we are forgiving. A rare lapse of judgment? A mistake made because the person is hurting in some way? Lonely? Has also been betrayed? Has the person suffered a loss and under unusual stress? We must also ask ourselves if the person who betrayed us is mostly guilty for being emotionally ignorant and incapable of understanding the harm done.

If any of the above is true, it might be easier to show compassion. As the quote at the beginning of this chapter suggests, people who have high self-esteem and healthy emotional and psychological lives do not intentionally betray other people. Those who have experienced the most harm themselves are most likely to do harm to others.

In a similar vein, several researchers of aggression and retaliation in the workplace argue that the target of injustice or wrongdoing decides whether or not the act was intentional. If the determination is that the act *was* intentional, that person is more likely to respond with retaliation and aggression.[3] At the extreme, we know that people such as Timothy McVeigh or Terry Nichols, those responsible for the devastating Oklahoma bombings, or the tragic instances of school bullying turning into bloody revenge such as Columbine, or the shootings at Virginia Tech, or the horrible attack on the World Trade Center were all motivated by revenge for the wrongs these people perceived had been done to them. For the less extreme wrongdoers, this rage is often embedded at an unconscious level. Some hurtful memories or incidents have been buried in psyches, only to turn up later in harmful behaviors. The point being, when someone harms us, sometimes compassion is the emotion we should be grasping for, rather than rage or revenge.[4]

However, there should be consequences for all behaviors: rewarding consequences for good behaviors, negative consequences for harmful and hurtful ones. Holding folks accountable for their wrongdoing is necessary, both for the good of society and for the individuals in question. Doing penance is cathartic, and compensating victims to the degree commensurate with their loss is the first step toward rehabilitation of the offender. Compassion, extended by those who have been wronged to those who have wronged them, does not lessen this requirement.

We Can't Observe Intentions

An important aspect of this discussion is that we can't really evaluate intentions; we can only evaluate observable behaviors. Assessing intentions is nearly impossible; we can only evaluate behaviors that might *hint* at someone's intentions. This is most likely the reason we make mistakes in assessing trustworthiness: We're never really certain of someone's intentions.

The law, however, *does* distinguish between intentional and unintentional harm; and intentional crimes are more harshly punished. Thus, our legal system has put into place a set of laws that protect its citizens more strongly from intentional harm than for crimes that are unintentional.[5] We should do the same in our personal relationships.

If the intention was to harm us, it will be much more difficult to forgive. If the harm was unintended, we might be more willing to forgive. So we must ask ourselves, to what do we attribute the betrayal?

Internal or External Attribution?

Social psychologists use Attribution Theory to examine explanations of others' behaviors by assessing whether the causes of the behavior were something internal (e.g., that's their personality) or external (a set of circumstances unique to the situation) and whether the behaviors are short-term (probably won't happen again) or more stable behaviors that last over time (they'll probably do it again).

If a bad behavior is attributed to stable, internal causes, we would predict the person to behave in the same way, across every situation, with all people, and over time.

We might think of this as personality, or a set of characteristics that predict how someone will act. In this case, people who behave badly in some situations would be predicted to behave badly in other situations. The bad behaviors are a part of their personalities. The same would be true of good behaviors. Assessing attribution allows us to make sense of the causes of another's behavior in ways that allow us to decide whether we want to continue a relationship with this person, and, if we do, the type of relationship we are willing to have. For example, if someone in our workplace has not prepared a report for our big presentation this afternoon (upon which our career was riding) and we are left with no presentation, we try to make sense of why that person did not come through. We might ask ourselves the following questions: Did the person lack the ability to do the task (internal attribution)? Did the person not take the effort necessary to complete the task (internal attribution)? Was the computer system faulty (external attribution)? Was the person up all night in the hospital with a sick child (external attribution)?

Searching all possible answers for the betrayal allows us to determine an appropriate course of action and how to base our future trust relationships with that person.

STEP 3: ANALYZE THE PERSONAL IMPACT OF THE BETRAYAL

Next, we must begin to evaluate the impact of the betrayal on our lives and assess whether the betrayal changed us in any way (good or bad) and question how important the relationship is to us.

We must also consider whether this one betrayal opened the door for other betrayals to follow and whether the personal effect is short or long term, severe or extreme.

STEP 4: ANALYZE THE REPERCUSSIONS FOR OTHERS

After we've articulated how the betrayal affected us personally, we must assess the repercussions on others. How public was the dispute? Who witnessed the betrayal and/or will suffer from it? Will a visible feud in the workplace make it more difficult for others to work with us? If I'm in partnership with this person, will the business collapse? Will my family suffer? If so, in what way? What does the public think of this situation?

Most of us can forgive others for acts of betrayal against ourselves more quickly than for acts of injustice against those we love (spouse, children, siblings, parents, close family/friends). This is evident when we consider the ramifications of a relationship-ending affair. The betrayed person may not only be angry and hurt for the personal loss but may also be devastated and angry at the betrayer who marred his or her own reputation in such a way that innocent children no longer have a trustworthy father or mother. The implications for children's development can be serious. As strange as it might seem, it is often not the actual act of betrayal that's the problem, but the fact that all future behaviors are now filtered through the prism of that act. The additional harm done to others, for whom we care, can make it extremely difficult to fully trust the betrayer again.

STEP 5: ASSESS WHETHER THE PERSON IS TRULY SORRY

The next step in deciding whether we will reconcile with someone who has betrayed us is determining whether the person is truly sorry for the betrayal. We might consider what the individual has said to us, or others, that indicates regret or remorse. What other signals (e.g., body language, behaviors) indicate regret or remorse? This is usually where we get good feedback from others, such as, *"So-and-so told me she was really sorry."* Is the person willing to pay a price for the harm done to us? The likelihood of reconciliation improves when the person is willing to be under the microscope while we engage in greater vigilance of his or her behavior and allow our emotions time to heal.

STEP 6: HAS THE PERSON LEARNED FROM THE MISTAKE AND WON'T DO IT AGAIN?

While being truly sorry for the behavior is especially important, an even more important part of reconciliation is in knowing the person has learned from his or her mistake and that the probability of harming us again is quite low. We'll want to contemplate whether the person has said anything to us or to others to indicate a lesson has been learned from this situation. This stage of the reconciliation process is all about what the person says and does that convinces us we won't be harmed again. Sometimes a simple *"I know I was wrong, and I'm not going to do that again"* is sufficient. Then, we wait to see with our own eyes as we observe their *actions* if the apology is sincere.

We should also weigh whether anything has been said/done that convinces us this person is capable of thinking beyond self-interest and has developed cognitively and emotionally from the experience. Is this perhaps not the first time we've been hurt by this person? Is this the final straw?

If we think the betrayer has learned from the mistake, we should establish a time period during which to monitor behaviors. If the person passes this test, then trust conditionally, until you have had time to build and create a new history of trust together.

PUT THE STEPS INTO ACTION

Now that we have the steps in mind that allow us to systematically assess whether or not we should give someone a second chance, let's put these steps into action, using the following stories taken from the interviews that were the foundation of this book. First, we'll read the vignettes, and then we'll use the steps outlined above to decide if the betrayer should be given a second chance.

BETRAYAL AT WORK

Roger, the president of a bank in the Midwest, tells of a breach of trust with Sam, a confidant in his workplace, with whom he formerly had implicit trust. Here's Roger's story:[6]

> Sam is a workplace contemporary of mine. We're nearly the same age and have other similarities. Sam is the VP of Organizational Effectiveness, the new buzzword for Human Resources. Well, Sam came into my office one day last week. I'm thinking we are "buds"—that I can say something to him in confidence and know that it will remain a confidence. So, I began to tell Sam that our company has been making huge mistakes by not getting more involved in commercial banking and real estate; that we were really missing the boat on this one. Admittedly, I became critical of my company's policies on these issues. It's also important to note that I'm often thought of as a bit of a maverick in this company. So, it was important to me this remain a confidential discussion, as I had already been labeled a trouble-maker. Some even already doubted my loyalty to the company. But I'm actually very loyal and want the bank to do better, yet, my criticism of policy and practices are often seen by others as not being a loyal team player, rather than an effort to make us better.
>
> For me, it was a travesty that our company was not more risk-taking in this regard. Our company has been going through this process called self-funding where we are having huge cuts in employees, using the money to reward those who really make a positive difference in the company in attempts to improve our bottom line. It was my opinion that the company was being mismanaged and there were better ways to spend our time and resources than on this self-funding project.
>
> I thought I was brainstorming with a trusted colleague. I soon found out this was not the case. This all happened on a Thursday. The next Tuesday, my boss's secretary came into my office and said my boss

wanted to see me. I knew it wasn't going to be good when he asked me to please close the door. My boss said, "Look, I think this guy, Sam, has it in for you. He and others think you aren't a team player and that you are attempting to cause a revolt within the company."

From my perspective, this was all outrageous, as I was only brainstorming. And I thought Sam was a trusted colleague. I thought I was even doing him a favor by giving him another perspective on the company. It was all very disappointing to see this get so twisted into something that was such a negative for me and the company.

Bottom line is, I will never trust this guy again. His intentions were obviously malicious. Even if he is sorry for what he did, I will never trust him again. I know I have to continue to work with him, but I will never trust him again.

This was all very disappointing to me. I thought we had a real comfort zone and that I could really trust him.

USING THE STEPS TO DISCUSS THE SAM/ROGER BETRAYAL

Step 1: Analyze the Breach of Trust

We begin by recognizing that the breach of trust in the first story is an enormous problem in Roger's work life. For one, Roger thinks this may ruin his career with this company and possibly his chance of gaining significant employment elsewhere. After all, who wants to work with someone who is perceived as disloyal to his boss and the company? We can even imagine Roger's embarrassment that he had confided in someone with such dangerous comments, comments that could be used to negatively affect his career. Sam made the betrayal public, and several senior executives, as well as the CEO, knew what had happened. The fact that several of Roger's peers also knew made the situation all the more painful and even humiliating.

Thus, this betrayal appears to be one big deal! It's a serious breach of trust and Roger needs to keep analyzing.

Step 2: Understand Why Sam Did It

It seems clear that Sam's betrayal of Roger was intentional. It would be hard to imagine this story to have slipped out during casual conversation. To Roger, Sam's intentions seem self-serving and selfish. Roger assumes that Sam did it to ingratiate himself with the boss at Roger's expense in an effort to get ahead faster. Few would think it is Roger's responsibility to understand why Sam did this and be supportive of Sam for his wrongdoing. Thus, Roger seems justified in assuming Sam's betrayal was intended to do him harm.

Roger assessed whether this act was consistent with Sam's personality. Roger had never known Sam to be untrustworthy but realized this may have been the first real test of Sam's character. Roger realized he didn't have enough information about Sam to know whether he had lied in other, similar situations or not. Consistent with what we know about trusted relationships, Roger made a trust judgment based on inadequate information. He wasn't certain whether he should attribute this betrayal to Sam's real personality or to some short-term lapse of judgment.

Roger questioned whether Sam was under some undue stress of his own that may have caused the bad behavior. Roger knew the company was under constraints and everyone was doing more with less. But for Roger, these constraints did not justify Sam's breach of trust.

Roger needs to continue on to Step 3 to adequately assess the possibility of reconciliation with Sam.

Step 3: Analyze the Personal Impact of the Betrayal

The betrayal had a significant impact on Roger. He began to question his ability to judge true friendships/confidants. He had thought Sam was his friend and would never betray him in this way. Not only his pride, but his self-image and self-esteem had been damaged by the betrayal. The relationship was important to Roger, in that Sam was a peer in the organization and he'd enjoyed being able to share confidences with him. While Roger could definitely live without Sam's friendship, he had enjoyed it immensely.

Step 4: Analyze the Repercussions for Others

Several important people in Roger's work life were aware of the breach, most importantly, the CEO of Roger's company, who had control of Roger's immediate work success. Roger was certain the CEO was disappointed that Roger had spoken of the company initiatives in such a derogatory manner. Several other senior executives were also aware of the betrayal. A public feud on the senior management team would create both significant short- and long-term problems for many people. The awkwardness of such a feud would negatively impact the efforts of the senior management team.

If the feud went too far and Roger or Sam were fired (more likely it would be Roger), Roger's family would also be negatively affected. The thought that what Sam had done would ultimately harm Roger's family was even more devastating to him.

The betrayal now seems extremely complex to Roger. On the one hand, he is livid and wants Sam out of his life. On the other hand, to continue this feud would surely hurt even more people, possibly including Roger's family.

More analysis was needed.

Step 5: Assess Whether Sam was Truly Sorry

Sam had never come to Roger to say he was sorry for breaching the confidence. Roger did approach Sam, in anger, in the hallway, and Sam merely noted he didn't tell the boss any untruths about what Roger had said. While this was probably true, he had still been disloyal to Roger. Needless to say, there was much office gossip about the feud, and it was clear to Roger from multiple sources that Sam was out to get him.

Step 6: Assess Whether Sam Has Learned from the Mistake and Will Not Do It Again

Given Sam wasn't even sorry for what he had done, it seems unlikely he had learned anything from the experience. It appeared probable that Sam would repeat the behavior if the occasion arose to benefit him in some way.

In this story, there seems to be little reason to expect that Roger should reconcile with Sam or give him a second chance at being a confidant. While Roger will want to eventually forgive Sam to relieve his own pain and anguish, it's time to examine Sam's role in his life. While others would suffer if Roger totally eliminated Sam from his life (team projects, maybe even poor relations with his boss), Roger must reframe his relationship with Sam as one of a colleague, but not a trusted confidant.

It will be difficult for Roger to forget what Sam did. In fact, he should never forget. However, he may forgive Sam, if he so chooses.

The betrayal has the potential of causing great distress to Roger and his career. Roger may also feel a bit foolish for having misplaced his trust in Sam. This does provide the opportunity for Roger to learn to be more observant with his trusted confidants and take the time to know someone better before divulging potentially dangerous information.

We should never make excuses for bad behavior. Those who are dishonest or disloyal to one person will be dishonest or disloyal to us when it suits their purposes. Given that Roger's life can proceed smoothly enough without having his former confidant in his inner circle, we can agree with Roger's decision to reframe the conditions of their working relationship into one in which Roger no longer shares intimate confidences with Sam.

The steps above helped Roger engage in full self-reflection of the betrayal; thus, he can feel greater confidence about his decision. It's time to cut his losses with Sam.

Betrayal in Our Personal Life

Tom had an affair, and his best friend, Steve, found out. Steve talked to Tom and told him to stop, but Tom didn't. Steve could see the shallowness of the affair, and he knew Tom had just lost his sense of good judgment. But Steve couldn't convince Tom at the time that it was wrong. Steve told Tom's wife about the affair. Tom was furious with Steve for betraying such a confidence as this. Tom thought he could work through this situation on his own. Steve knew Tom couldn't handle it; he had begun to tell lies to everyone around him, most importantly to himself.

Like many who become involved in an affair, Tom thought others didn't know and thought his was unique and special. He'd become blinded to the humiliation and harm he was doing to himself and others. Steve knew that continuing this affair could ruin Tom's marriage and ultimately tarnish Tom's image as a man of integrity.

At first, Tom was furious with Steve. His life came tumbling down; his wife was enraged, and he didn't have Steve as his best friend any longer. How could Tom trust someone who would reveal a secret such as this?

Thanks to Steve, however, Tom began to see that the affair was one of convenience. Tom admitted it was fun, a short-term fix, and a real escape from the realities of life, but he was betraying the person he trusted most in life, his wife. Tom realized that part of the intrigue with his new love interest was that he could see her when he wanted to and didn't have to see her when he chose not to. He knew he had to untangle himself from the life he had created, and he knew it wasn't going to be easy. Tom felt pretty crummy.

It took a long time, but he and his wife created a new and better life for themselves, and Tom realized that Steve really was a best friend. Steve wasn't afraid to tell Tom when he was doing something terribly wrong and he wasn't afraid to risk their friendship by doing what was right to help Tom by telling Tom's wife about the affair.

After his initial anger at Steve for betraying him by revealing a confidence to his wife, he soon realized Steve's intentions were honorable. He only wanted to help Tom and his family. Steve knew how much Tom valued his sense of self-worth and his family, and Steve also knew that, for Tom, living life as an untrustworthy person was simply wrong for both him and his family.

USING THE STEPS TO DISCUSS THE STEVE/ BEST FRIEND BETRAYAL

Step 1: Analyze the Breach of Trust

When we examine this *best friend* story, we see again that the breach of trust was devastating. Telling a best friend's wife that her husband is having an affair is a serious matter. Given the nature of the problem, many people became aware of the breach. The betrayal had huge implications for Tom's personal and family life, probably even his work life, given the major disruption this betrayal caused.

Step 2: Understand Why Steve Did It

While this breach of trust was egregious, Tom came to understand that it was not done with malicious intent, and what Tom had first thought of as a betrayal, he now realized was the ultimate display of unselfishness on Steve's part. Rather than being emotionally ignorant, a possibility noted in Step 2, the betrayal was one of emotional and cognitive strength. Tom realized that Steve had betrayed him for his own good.

Step 3: Analyze the Personal Impact of the Betrayal

The betrayal had an enormous personal impact on Tom. It forced him to realize he had been fooling himself for a long time. Tom had pretended to himself that he wasn't really lying when he misled people about where he was and who he was with. It all just *happened*. For Tom, it was as if he allowed himself to think he didn't have control over his own behavior, rather than a personal choice he was making that was harmful to himself and other important people in his life. It seemed so much more innocent at the time than it did when it was all over.

Tom was humiliated at his behavior and his selfishness. He was remorseful about what he had done and how he had allowed himself to be weak and selfish. Steve's act of betrayal forced Tom to assess the relationships in his life and prioritize them in ways that made his decision of what to do and how to behave much clearer. *How* Tom chose to conduct his life was the central issue. He chose the path of integrity over one of selfishness and predictable harm to himself and others.

In the story above, it's pretty easy to see that the best friend's intentions were honorable and Steve was trying to help resolve a situation that had the potential of ruining Tom's life. It's much easier to forgive someone for a betrayal when we know the intention was to be helpful. It is much more difficult, if not impossible, to forgive someone when the intentions are selfish and seem to be directed at harming us. It is in these instances that we have to work harder to understand why someone betrayed us and decide whether we will be willing to repair the relationship.

Step 4: Analyze the Repercussions for Others

The breach of trust also had the potential to affect many other people: his wife, innocent children, their friends, neighbors, extended family, and the woman involved in the affair. Steve recognized this possibility and wanted to be assured that Tom would be able to be reinstated as a man of honor. By revealing the affair to Tom's wife, Steve took the risk that Tom's children would find out. He would be part of the story. He would be the one who had stolen from the children their image of their father as a man of integrity.

In this instance, the betrayal of the best friend was not particularly public, but the affair was known to many more than Tom had realized.

Step 5: Determine If Steve Was Truly Sorry

It seemed clear from this interview that Steve was very sorry for all of the turmoil in Tom's life, but not for what he had done. He didn't have to be. In this case, not being sorry is acceptable. Steve's willingness to risk his friendship with Tom and his family was done unselfishly and with great care and concern for those involved. Many people would rather take the easy way out and say what Tom wanted to hear, instead of what would help him be a better person. As noted in the life insights, "Good guys won't let me be bad."

Step 6: Did Steve Learn a Lesson? Will He Make the Same Mistake Again?

Steve probably learned a lesson; hopefully, Tom did too. Yes, Steve would probably put himself at risk again to save Tom from himself and help him be a good guy. We should all be so lucky to have people like this in our lives.

So, Should Tom Reconcile With Steve?

Tom thanked Steve over and again for helping him be a better guy by not letting him live a life of deceit. Steve had shown Tom, on multiple occasions, that he was an unselfish person and would do what was right for Tom, regardless of any negative implications for himself. Steve warned Tom that he was being a jerk to both his wife and even to the person with whom he was having the affair.

For Steve, being deceitful and encouraging someone else to be deceitful isn't a sign of a loving relationship but rather a sign of greed and selfishness. Tom also noted that while Steve encouraged him to give up the affair, Steve (the ultimate good guy) also showed him that the most important thing was that Tom should stop being deceitful. If he wanted to leave his wife and be with the other woman, Tom should tell his wife of this wish, be honest, and treat everyone in the situation with more respect. As noted in the earlier insights, we all deserve the respect of the truth. Regardless of whom Tom chose, in the long run, being a person of integrity was best for Tom, his family, and even the other woman.

The two examples above have given us some practice in using the steps to decide whether to give someone a second chance. I encourage you to go through each of the steps above if, or when, you experience betrayal.

Now, let's assume we've decided we want to reconcile with someone who has betrayed us. How does that reconciliation actually occur? What do we do? How do we behave/react/cope during the reconciliation?

NOTES

1.   Dennis S. Reina and Michelle L. Reina, *Trust and Betrayal in the Workplace* (San Francisco: Berrett-Koehler Publishers, 2006).

2.   The names of this person and the school have been changed to protect anonymity.

3.   J. H. Neuman and R. A. Baron, "Aggression in the Workplace: A Social-Psychological Perspective," in *Counterproductive Work Behavior: Investigations of Actors and Targets*, ed. S. Fox and P. E. Spector, 13–40 (Washington, DC: APA Press, 2004).

4.   Mariah Burton Nelson (www.mariahburtonnelson.com/forgivework.htm).

5.   Stephen M. R. Covey, *The Speed of Trust* (New York: Free Press, 2006).

6.   The names of these individuals have been changed to protect their anonymity.

Chapter 19

How to Cope

Our distrust is very expensive.

—Ralph Waldo Emerson

WITH ANY RELATIONSHIP, even those with the good guys, we sometimes have to recover from an altercation that knocks us off our feet. Someone betrays us, asks for forgiveness, we give it, and we may even reconcile, but what happens to us psychologically because of this betrayal? How do we cope once we've decided to reconcile with someone who has betrayed us? There are several tips to follow, once we've made the decision to repair a relationship and begin the reconciliation process. Even with the *best* of good guys, when they've disappointed us, sometimes we have to learn how to cope. Coping is all about taking our time and not rushing to make a life-altering decision until we've gained a clearer perspective.

A COOLING-OFF PERIOD COMES FIRST

As we begin reconciliation, it's best to begin by retreating a few steps, being quiet for a while, and treading carefully with any new information or confidences we share with the person who betrayed us. Being quiet helps us think things through and shelters us from saying or doing anything rash, which could make the situation worse. Most of us aren't able to think clearly when we are upset or emotionally hurt. This holds true for either a work-related or a personal breach of trust. We just need to back off for a while, allow time to evolve, do a little more learning, and permit ourselves to become more centered before we make any major life decisions about the person who has betrayed us. As one senior executive put it:

WE NEED MORE DATA

There are times now when I know a decision isn't ready to be made; we need more data. We need more experience, we need more time, we need more analysis, and we need more something. I've learned that from my divorce; don't make life decisions unless you are fully prepared. And I wasn't. I didn't have enough time, didn't know my former wife well enough, and wasn't mature enough at the time.

—Robert Pilsner, COO, Multinational Manufacturing Company[1]

WE SHOULD'VE LEARNED IT LONG AGO

The need for a cooling-off period reminds me of the ways our daughter-in-law, Brandy, helps our grandchildren, Brayden and Brooke, work through their frustrations, as they learn to cope with the negative aspects and disappointments of their lives. When Brayden or Brooke is about to have a temper tantrum because they can't have something they want, or someone or something has disappointed them, or someone hasn't shown them the attention they want at that particular time, Brandy distracts them and places them in a different environment. Then, when they return to a peaceful state of equilibrium, Brandy will have a short conversation with them about sharing, being nice, dealing with disappointment, or whatever the real problem had been.

Brandy is aware that most of us can't be rational when we're upset (regardless of the cause, or frankly our age); we simply can't think clearly in that state of confusion. Continuing to discuss the problem when we are in this state is a waste of everybody's time and energy and can easily spiral out of control, if not handled with grace and finesse, regardless of our age! So, it's often important for us to gain a little distance from a problem before we attempt to solve it; otherwise, we can create an even bigger problem than before.

It's obvious that just walking away and achieving equilibrium isn't the only key. We have to then return to the problem when we have better perspective and a clearer mind. It works great on our grandchildren, Brayden and Brooke. It's an important coping strategy for us, as well. Yet, somewhere along the way, we may have forgotten this, or maybe, we never, ever learned it!

The decision will come, but it just takes time.

REACQUAINT YOURSELF WITH THIS PERSON

The reconciliation actually creates a new relationship with the person who betrayed us. Given that the breach may have been enormous, this new information changes our idea of who this person actually is. It takes time to assimilate this new information and make new decisions based upon this new understanding. In effect, we have to reacquaint ourselves with this person.

As we continue on this path to reconciliation, we should refer frequently to the Toolkit (Chapter 9) to reassess this person's trustworthiness. Over time, as we gain more and more objectivity, we will more clearly see how/why/when the trust we placed in this person changed. We now have new information about this person's behavior and character that we didn't have before. The information may have been there, but perhaps we just chose to ignore it. Now, we must use this new information to help us reframe our relationship. During the initial coping stages, we may feel less vulnerable if we trust, but with a degree of vigilance.

CONTINUAL VIGILANCE IS IMPORTANT

If the breach was monumental and the person a trusted confidant, we must begin our new relationship with purposeful vigilance. This might entail periodically checking up on the individual, asking friends or other confidants about the person's behavior, and observing closely any behaviors that might hint at a regression toward yet another betrayal. It's difficult to determine how long and how severe the vigilance should be, but we should establish periodic proof-points that allow us to reassess whether we want to continue with the reconciliation. While previously checking up on a confidant's behaviors may never have crossed our minds, the betrayal has taught us that we must begin. Starting down this path of reconciliation doesn't mean we must complete the journey. At any stage or at any time we think the relationship is too time-consuming or the benefits stop outweighing the negatives, we can choose to end it.

Rich Hoskins offers a helpful insight:

SHOW ME AND YOU HAVE EARNED MY TRUST

In the end, I still live by the principle, "Show me and you have earned my trust." If I get burned, I can forgive, but generally will not provide much trust to that individual in the future. If I have to work with them again, I do it with extreme caution and try to build in limits to the risks associated with failure. Generally, I seek ways not to have further dealings with them.

—Richard Hoskins III, CEO, Colborne Corporation

AT WHAT POINT DO WE QUIT BEING VIGILANT?

During this time of vigilance, we can observe behaviors that suggest the person is truly sorry, has repented, and learned from the mistake. This is a time when words mean little, and behavior means everything. As Doug Conant, former CEO of Campbell Soup, told me, when we have a relationship problem:

"We have to *behave* ourselves out of a problem, not *talk* our way out of the problem."

At some point, however, we have to ask ourselves how much time are we willing to put into being vigilant? When will we quit? Will we ever? Is the relationship worth the time/effort to continue? When the behavior and actions prove the worth of the words, then and only then is it time.

SOMETHING RE-BONDS US

When/if the relationship becomes one of full trust again, it is often because something happens during the reconciliation period that re-bonds us. The betrayer does something, or a bunch of little *somethings*, that reveals a willingness to make personal sacrifices that benefit us, regardless of the personal consequences. The individual confirms, through caring behavior, as well as words, the lesson has been learned. When this happens, the new relationship can be even stronger than the former one because we've been able to work through a very difficult problem in a way that benefits us both and creates an even stronger trust bond than before the betrayal.

SUMMARY

This chapter has shown us how difficult it is to cope with someone when we've had a serious breach of trust. As the quote at the beginning of Chapter 17 notes: "Forgiveness is an attribute of the strong." It's true—we have to be strong in mind and spirit in order to forgive someone who has betrayed us. Yet, reconciliations may be easier when we can begin to understand why someone did something harmful to us. We may ultimately have an even better relationship with this person than ever before, as we spend time learning to better understand each other.

We've learned a systematic process that can help us through this difficult time, a process that helps us assess whether we should even consider reconciliation. If we do, we've learned how to cope during the reconciliation process. We've learned that we should always forgive, but rarely forget. We've learned we must analyze before we do reconcile, and we've learned that we must take our time. We've learned that, when we have a workplace or personal life relationship problem, contrary to our quick-fix-it and instant-gratification society norms, it's beneficial to take a time-out in the adult world, a time-out that we place on ourselves.

Now, let's take a look at whether *we* are good guys or not . . .

NOTE

1. This name has been changed to protect anonymity.

Chapter 20

Looking Inward: Am I a Good Guy?

Courage doesn't always roar. Sometimes courage is that little voice at the end of the day that says 'I'll try again tomorrow.'

—Mary Anne Radmacher

SOMETIMES I'M THE BAD GUY

As important as it was for us to assess the trustworthiness of our colleagues, friends, and family, perhaps it's even *more* important for us to understand how we can be better guys *ourselves*! As my son-in-law, Joe Gittleman, told me, "Sometimes *I'm* the bad guy." (I'm pretty sure he was speaking of himself. Surely he didn't mean *me*, did he?)

Most people want to be good guys, but occasionally even good guys make mistakes and act like bad guys. Few good guys, however, exhibit bad behaviors over a long period of time. The good guy's conscience wouldn't let that happen. For most of us, the journey to *good guydom* takes time, and the hope is that our mistakes get fewer and fewer and less and less distressing along the way. Here's a story from someone who experienced this firsthand:

THERE WAS NO SERPENT SPEAKING FROM THE TREES

Like everyone else, I witnessed with disgust and anger the seeming deterioration of business ethics that came to light with Enron, Worldcom, Parmalat, Citibank Japan, and other corporate deceptions. I asked the same questions as did others: "What is wrong with these people? How do people with such bad judgment end up in positions of responsibility? What is wrong with the training and education of executives?"

But such questions also provide a false comfort. They suggest that the problem is in others. Recently, events in my own life confronted me with a less comfortable truth. I contemplated having an affair. This was not existential musing; it was a specific temptation. It was not because someone undermined my good sense or engaged in remarkable seduction that could not be resisted; it was something that appealed to me. There was no serpent speaking to me from the tree. The apple just seemed like it would taste so very good. If I could consider so basic a betrayal of the person closest to me, my spouse, and in violation of my vows and commitments, how could I claim moral superiority to people engaged in arcane manipulation of numbers to the detriment of those to whom they had only a commercial obligation?

I owe it to my wife and family to note that I did not pursue the possibility of the affair. It is a choice I am glad I made, but I realize how easily I could have chosen differently. I'm grateful that the person I nearly became involved with was a thoughtful, perceptive person who understood that doing so would hurt a lot of innocent people needlessly. She, in essence, became a friend that wouldn't let me do something that was harmful to the people I care for so much.

Most of us face temptations, whether it is to fudge quality standards to meet production quotas, engage in legerdemain to make the quarterly numbers, or something in our personal lives. These are challenges we all face. Some succumb and some do not, and that raises the question of what makes people choose to go the right way. What is it in the person, situation, or community surrounding us that leads to righteous choices? It is not some breed of people different from ourselves, who are engaged in the wrongdoing that we all eagerly deplore. I, too, am curious what makes people be "good guys." I feel comfortable that the answer is, in part, in choosing to spend one's time with people of integrity, people who won't let me make mistakes that hurt me and those I love. They won't let me make mistakes that I may regret.

—Grant Armstrong, Executive VP Marketing, Vonaggers[1]

The story above is a sincere and honest account depicting the power of taking personal responsibility for, and being reflective about, our behaviors. As the story reminds us, there is really no *serpent speaking from the tree;* it's just our own voice and our own decisions about how we want to live our lives.

Perhaps the ultimate test of personal responsibility is to take a hard look at our own behaviors and assess just how trustworthy we are.

HOW TRUSTWORTHY ARE YOU? TAKE THE TEST!

Let's do a quick refresher of the characteristics of a trustworthy person. These are summarized in Table 20.1, but this time, *you* are the focus. Just as you did when you assessed the trustworthiness of friends, family, and colleagues, ask yourself each question in the Trust Rules Self-Questionnaire and then rate yourself in each area on a scale of 1–10. You will arrive at a systematic assessment of your own perceived trustworthiness.

Table 20.1 Trust Rules Self-Questionnaire

Answer each question by rating yourself on a scale of 1–10, 1 meaning you **do not** have this characteristic and 10 meaning you **do** have this characteristic. Place your rating on the space provided at the beginning of each question. Add each rating to get the Total Score. The higher the number, the more trustworthy you perceive yourself to be.

Value	Trait	I Definitely Do Not Have This Characteristic								I Definitely Have This Characteristic	
	Do you have a history that demonstrates good values?	1 2 3 4	5	6	7	8	9	10			
	Are you likely to respond in a healthy way, when things go wrong?	1 2 3 4	5	6	7	8	9	10			
	Do you admit and learn from mistakes?	1 2 3 4	5	6	7	8	9	10			
	Do you have a self-awareness that demonstrates you know how your behavior affects others?	1 2 3 4	5	6	7	8	9	10			
	Do you treat everyone the same, regardless of their level in the hierarchy (work or social)?	1 2 3 4	5	6	7	8	9	10			
	Do you demonstrate consistent good behaviors?	1 2 3 4	5	6	7	8	9	10			
	Do you have positive qualities, other than good looks, a good education, and wealth?	1 2 3 4	5	6	7	8	9	10			
	Do you never take advantage of others using your own good looks, education, or wealth?	1 2 3 4	5	6	7	8	9	10			
	Do you admit when you don't know something?	1 2 3 4	5	6	7	8	9	10			
	Do you demonstrate absolute integrity?	1 2 3 4	5	6	7	8	9	10			
	Do you genuinely consider others in your life?	1 2 3 4	5	6	7	8	9	10			
	Do you voluntarily, in healthy ways, tell others when they are doing something wrong?	1 2 3 4	5	6	7	8	9	10			
	Do you help others be better people?	1 2 3 4	5	6	7	8	9	10			
	Would others introduce you to their family and other trusted confidants?	1 2 3 4	5	6	7	8	9	10			
	Are you likely to respond in a healthy way, when you don't get your way?	1 2 3 4	5	6	7	8	9	10			
	Do you hold yourself to the same standards you establish for others?	1 2 3 4	5	6	7	8	9	10			
	Do you do the right thing?	1 2 3 4	5	6	7	8	9	10			
	Do you stick by others in bad/tough times?	1 2 3 4	5	6	7	8	9	10			
	Do you speak the same of people, whether they are in your presence or not?	1 2 3 4	5	6	7	8	9	10			
	Are you likely to share resources (time, space, money, friends)?	1 2 3 4	5	6	7	8	9	10			

_____ **TOTAL SCORE (Total possible score between 20 and 200)**

Figure 20.1   How Trustworthy Are You Scale

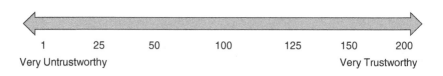

| 1 | 25 | 50 | 100 | 125 | 150 | 200 |

Very Untrustworthy   Very Trustworthy

Based on your Total Score from the Trust Rules Self-Questionnaire, place yourself on the Trust Rules Self-Scale. The higher the number, the more trustworthy you perceive yourself to be.

When you've entered your Total Score on the Trust Rules Self-Questionnaire (Table 20.1), place your Total Score on the How Trustworthy Are You Scale continuum (Figure 20.1) and see just where you lie. You can now answer the question, how good a guy are *you*?

If you are honest in your analysis, you might be surprised to learn that you aren't as trustworthy as you think you are. This can come as a bit of a shock!

We've learned that being untrustworthy doesn't only mean making big mistakes; it can also mean being untrustworthy in many small ways that accumulate to weaken a trusted and valued relationship. What are these little items that add up? You don't return phone calls, you gossip, speak harshly, are impatient, engage in behind-the-scenes manipulation with a personal agenda, are needlessly critical, etc. Ouch!

These small breaches of trust, especially personal criticisms, are even more harmful when spoken to those most close to you, those who are most vulnerable and who trust most that you won't emotionally or physically harm them. As the small breaches of trust (frequent criticisms, impatience, lack of kindness) accumulate, they erode the trust others have placed in you. The cumulative effect is oftentimes as dangerous as a major betrayal.

It takes courage to apply the Trust Rules Self-Questionnaire to yourself and seriously consider your own level of trustworthiness. I would venture a guess that only good guys will even *take* the test and bad guys won't even bother assessing how they measure up (or will try to explain away a low score). Typically, it's the good guy who wants to do better, every day. The bad guys neither recognize nor care that they have a problem.

Once you've completed this task, you can determine your weakest traits as depicted in the Trust Rules Self-Questionnaire and develop strategies to help you become more trustworthy.

WE'RE RESPONSIBLE FOR OUR OWN CHOICES

While none of us can relive the past, if we want to be good guys, we must use our regrets as tools to shape our future behaviors in positive ways.

So, the first step on the road to *good guydom* is to examine our past behaviors. If we can confidently say that our set of principles, or *credo*, is strong, and we are able to live our values in both easy and difficult times, we are among the few really good guys. If we've developed a set of principles and learned from past mistakes, we're much further along the road to being a good guy. If, however, we realize we are easily, negatively influenced by others, it's time to use this awareness when encountering those gray areas of our lives.

IF I'M RESPONSIBLE FOR MY CHOICES, WHAT CAN I DO TO BECOME MORE TRUSTWORTHY?

Take the Trust Rules Self-Questionnaire. The ultimate self-improvement project is asking yourself, "What can I do to make myself more trustworthy?" One way to become more trustworthy would be to identify the gaps in the Trust Rules Self-Questionnaire, reflect on areas needing improvement, and then develop an action plan to address those gaps. It would be even better if a trusted confidant would also do this for you. In the best of all worlds, you could assess your own trustworthiness based on the Trust Rules Self-Questionnaire in Table 20.1, and then compare that to others' perspective of you. Then, work to improve those areas of weakness.

It's awkward, at first, doing this exercise with others. It's not easy telling others they aren't perfectly trustworthy and even harder to hear it yourself. The experience has to be undertaken by people who seriously want to become more trusted individuals. When my family and I took the Trust Rules Toolkit and reported on each other's trustworthiness, we began delicately. Then, as the process continued, we began to trust each other to know that the feedback was intended as helpful and that only someone who really cared about us would be willing to share this experience.

We laughed, had a good time, and were fascinated to see the trust grow among us, as the process unfolded. We learned a great deal about ourselves and about each other during the experience. It was just what I had hoped for when I first undertook this project of learning about trust. I'd hoped the process would be provocative enough to compel all of us to discuss the importance of change to our lives. More importantly, I wanted to help everyone learn more about whom to trust, how to become more trustworthy, and especially to learn the importance of trust to any meaningful relationship.

As we've seen, the first step in the process is developing awareness. You have to be able to assess your own strengths and weaknesses objectively, as they relate to trustworthiness, and be prepared to hear objective feedback from others as well.

BECOME AN OBJECTIVE SELF-ASSESSOR OF YOUR BEHAVIOR

Are you able to step outside your interactions with others and become, in essence, a clone of yourself, observing your own behaviors in objective ways?

Can you reflect on whether your behavior is fair? Can you be mindful of the impact your behaviors might have on those who are important to you, as well as on others? As our philosopher friend Immanuel Kant might ask, "Can you imagine how the world would be, if everyone behaved the way you do? Would it be a better world, if everyone treated each other the way you just treated your colleague, friend, spouse, and neighbor?" If you reflect on this, you may realize you've been thoughtless or haven't considered the impact of your actions upon others. If you're cognitively and emotionally mature, you can rectify this situation, apologize, and become more mindful of your future actions.

Objective self-awareness occurs when you are able to view the role you play in causing actions and their consequences—when you are able to view your actions as others might see them. Unfortunately, most of us have a self-perception bias that works to our detriment and ultimately to the detriment of others.

Those who are not able to be objectively self-aware are more likely to blame a situation on someone else or affix an "*it just happened mentality*" to any problem.

Research has shown, however, that the next best thing to our having an objective self-awareness is surrounding ourselves with people who make us more self-aware. When individuals are given feedback that demonstrates their role in actions and consequences, they are more likely to attribute a greater source of the problem to their own actions.

Unfortunately, we all have varying levels of willingness to listen and absorb feedback from others. Those of us who are willing, however, are better equipped to view our behaviors as an impartial observer[2] would and then act on that feedback to positively change our behaviors.

SURROUND YOURSELF WITH PEOPLE WHO WILL GIVE YOU ACCURATE FEEDBACK

We can never forget the personal responsibility aspect of our bad behaviors, but research and our mothers' proclamations (birds of a feather flock together!) clearly support the claim that others have tremendous influence on us, whether we are consciously or unconsciously aware of it. During those not-so-black-and-white-times in your life, if you choose your friends/confidants carefully, they can help you make better decisions. They won't let you be bad!

Even those of us who are not Buddhists can turn to their teachings for important and practical insights of how to live peaceful and happy lives. One of my favorites is the story that encourages us to associate with the *wise*. In this story, Ananda, a principal disciple of Buddha, commented to Buddha: "This is half of the holy life, lord: having admirable people as friends, companions, and colleagues." Buddha replied, "Don't say that, Ananda. Don't say that. Having admirable people as friends, companions, and colleagues is actually the whole of life."

According to Buddhist teachings, one's progress along the path to enlightenment hinges on choosing friendships that help us grow in positive ways. Even Buddha offers advice on how to distinguish good advisers from bad ones. For Buddha, bad guys are without shame and moral dread; they are unmindful and are devoid of wisdom.[3]

We can all imagine how our lives could have been different, had we made different choices at crucial junctures. Would those choices have been easier, if we'd surrounded ourselves with people of integrity to help us make positive choices during those difficult times? Or, conversely, had we not surrounded ourselves with people of integrity, would we have fallen prey to those negative influences that may have encouraged us to engage in destructive behaviors?

Tim Storey, author of the book, *Comeback and Beyond*, puts it prudently. He says, we have the choice to walk with wise people and stack up on wisdom or we can become a companion of fools and our lives will unravel.[4]

The research of author and professor Laura Roberts[5] supports this claim. For Roberts, surrounding ourselves with people of integrity has important positive implications on our own behaviors. She warns, however, that positive relationships are only positive when each party provides candid feedback to the other. Delusions of grandeur and self-destructive behaviors can occur when our confidants only provide us with positive feedback.

Dr. Tom Dicke, our physician-philosopher, considers the importance of feedback early in our lives:

SOMEONE HAS TO CARE ENOUGH TO GIVE YOU FEEDBACK

During adolescence, we are all trying to develop an identity. We try on a few different hats, see what works, and get feedback on our good and bad behaviors. Those that successfully master this stage mature and move beyond adolescence to realize that lying, cheating, and betraying others isn't *cool*. We've tested those behaviors to some degree during adolescence and, if we're successful, and, if someone cared enough to give us feedback, we learned these behaviors were bad.

Some, however, get stuck in that adolescent stage and continue to do these unethical things all their lives, because they didn't learn as teenagers (or some other stage of their life) that it is wrong. They probably never had "confidants," as you call them, but especially parents or siblings, or teachers that took the time and care to give them good feedback about the importance of being honorable, unselfish, and reflective about their behavior. It's the one thing for which I thank my mom and dad. They cared enough about me and had the cognitive and emotional strength to teach me that my integrity was something no one, but I, could ever take away from myself. To this day, I guard my integrity with my life.

A PERSONAL STORY

I remember a time in our family life when our children, Angie and Brad, were pre-teenagers and teenagers. We had moved from a small, rural community to a major metropolitan city—an international one at that, Montreal, Quebec, where French is the primary language in the schools and the community. Our children (and my husband and I, too) worked to make new friends, new confidants. Being a teenager, attempting to find an identity, and doing so without those former trusted friends and peers makes being a teenager (and being a parent of teenagers) particularly challenging.

Dropping them off at their new schools that first day, I felt remorse for taking them from their old comfortable environment and friends. There was that pit in my stomach that only a parent can identify with, as I fully understood the challenges they would face, and knew there was little I could do to help them during these first days at their new schools. I'm proud of the way they mastered those challenges. However, as I look back on this time in their lives, I can recapture that feeling in an instant and I recognize even more fully how important our friends and confidants are to our development, regardless of our age. Without these anchors that help guide us and hold us to our core values, anyone can become a rudderless ship.

YOU EXAMINE THE ROLE YOU PLAY WHEN YOU'VE BEEN BETRAYED

It takes two to make a relationship, and it's rare when both parties in a betrayal don't share some degree of the responsibility. Thus, when/if you are betrayed at work or in your personal life, you must consider the role you played in that betrayal:

- Is there something about the way you interact with people, or the person who betrayed you, that gave them few other choices?

- Do you have such an unforgiving nature that you make it extremely difficult for people to bring you bad news, thus forcing them to keep things from you so that the small problem becomes huge?

- Are your standards and expectations so incredibly high that no one could meet them?

- Are you just too trusting and lack a balance between trusting too much and not trusting enough (*per* Erikson's theory noted in earlier chapters)?

- Is there something about your behavior that seems to cry out, "Take advantage of me!" Do you appear too desperate for friendship, acceptance, or love? Do you think you have something to gain from playing the victim?

- And, finally, are you just too innocent/naïve to suspect someone might betray you?

As many counselors and workplace coaches acknowledge, there is rarely a conflict or betrayal where only one person is at fault. In order to safeguard against future situations, it's important to do a personal inventory and assess the role you may have played. Work to understand how to be more perceptive, so you'll notice when those around you might be slipping away from a trusted status.

WELL, ARE YOU TRUSTWORTHY?

So let's return to the question, *"Are you trustworthy?"* The truth is, only your family, friends, and colleagues can answer that. You can take the Trust Rules Self-Questionnaire and think you are. You can cite examples, and you can feel good about your Trust Rules Total Score or you can recognize weak links in your behavior and character and work to make positive changes.

When I first took the Trust Rules Self-Questionnaire test, I kept going back, trying to figure out ways to make myself score better. Well, maybe I am an 8 on integrity instead of a 7. I try really hard to be honest in every conversation. Maybe I am an 8 on the self-awareness factor. Lots of people seem to come to me for advice. I wanted so much to be a really, really good guy, by the standard I had set for others. When total honesty finally hit me, I recognized that the percentages and numbers weren't important; it was the behaviors and actions behind the numbers that meant something. If I really wanted to be a better *guy*, I had to be honest with myself and recognize that I'm just as fallible as anyone else. To achieve *good guydom*, I needed to objectively assess my own strengths and weaknesses and vow to have the courage to try to be a better person tomorrow.

DO YOU TRUST YOURSELF?

Trusting yourself is more than trusting that you will be trustworthy to others. Trusting yourself also means you trust *yourself*. When you've shown yourself, through your interactions with others, that you are trustworthy, honest, and do not harm those you care for, work with, and spend your daily lives with, you develop a self-image that rewards you with a sense of inner peace.

Those times when you find yourself being temporarily selfish, self-centered, thoughtless, and perhaps not totally honest with others, you'll notice that it takes more time to do what you have to do. You struggle with the negative experiences you are currently creating and make no forward progress. It's in your power, however, to turn away from this detour and regain the highway of *good guydom*. More in the next chapter.

SUMMARY

Not every instance of untrustworthiness is of earth-shattering proportions. Most often, we are both the perpetrators and victims of our own duplicity. The Trust Rules Self-Questionnaire is a valuable tool to help us make good decisions to become more trustworthy. Then, fully armed, we will be prepared to tackle the larger issues that the workplace and our personal relationships demand of us. In the next chapter, we'll discuss more about the importance of trusting yourself and its importance on the journey to good guydom.

NOTES

1.   The name of this person has been changed to protect his anonymity.

2.   Linda K. Stroh, Gregory B. Northcraft, and Margaret A. Neale, *Organizational Behavior: A Management Challenge* (New Jersey: Lawrence Erlbaum, 2002), 46.

3.   Bhikkhu Bodhi, *Association with the Wise* (Buddhist Publication Society, http://wanderling.tripod.com/wise.html, March 1, 2007).

4.   Tim Storey, *Comeback & Beyond: How to Turn Your Setback into Your Comeback* (Goshen: Harrison House, 2010).

5.   Laura Morgan Roberts, "From Proving to Becoming: How Positive Relationships Create a Context for Self-Discovery and Self-Actualization," in *Exploring Positive Relationships at Work: Building a Theoretical and Research Foundation*, ed. Jane Dutton and Belle Rose Ragins, 29–45 (New Jersey: Lawrence Erlbaum, 2007).

Chapter 21

Can You Trust Yourself?

This above all: to thine own self be true. And it must follow, as the night the day,
Thou canst not then be false to any man.

—Shakespeare

THIS BOOK HAS EXPLORED WAYS to help sort people we can trust from those we can't, as we work toward building more authentic relationships. An equally, if not more important relationship, however, is the one we have with ourselves. Positive relationships with others are built upon conversation, feedback, and two-way interactions. When those conversations and interactions are trustworthy (the ones with the good guys in our lives), we typically find the best relationships of all. The same is true of the relationship we have with ourselves. When the reflective conversations we have with ourselves and the resulting explorations into behaviors and actions are honest and trustworthy, we are likely to be more well-adjusted, content, and peaceful human beings— *Good Guys!* Just as we trust the good guys in our lives, the ultimate good guys trust *themselves* to keep the promises and commitments they make to themselves.

A NEW QUESTION

Have you ever asked yourself, "Do *I* trust *me*?" Probably not, but you might benefit from pondering this seemingly paradoxical question. So, go ahead and ask yourself that question: "Do I trust myself?" Let's examine this question and its relevance to the importance of trust in our lives. Remember, this isn't asking the question, "Can *others* trust you?" but rather, "Can *you* trust *yourself*?" You might be surprised by what you find.

COLLECT THE DATA

The first step in answering this question is to collect the data. Examine your behaviors and the promises and commitments you make to yourself. Have you followed through on those promises? In order for this examination to be successful, you must obtain reliable and valid data. Don't evade the truth or make excuses. Be honest with yourself; no one else can answer this question for you.

In Chapter 9, when we assessed the trustworthiness of our confidants, we discovered how easy it is to rationalize bad behavior: It was really the other person's fault, or it just happened, or I had no other choice. This can be a particularly seductive temptation when reflecting on ourselves. Instead, we need to just measure, by our actions and behaviors and not our words, thoughts, or intentions, whether we have kept promises and commitments to ourselves.

Think of the five most recent promises you have made to yourself. Here are some examples to get you thinking:

1. "I'm going to lose 15 pounds."
2. "I'm going to be more patient and not lose my temper."
3. "I'm going to listen more carefully to people and not interrupt them."
4. "I'm going to learn a new language."
5. "I am going to quit this affair tonight."
6. "I am going to volunteer for a charitable cause."
7. "I am going to quit charging and only pay cash."
8. "I am going to eat less for dinner, because I splurged at lunch."
9. "I'm going to spend more time with my family."
10. "I'm going to read a book on trust."

Okay, so there aren't only five examples. The possibilities are endless. Now, take a moment and write down just five promises you've made to *yourself*. How did you do? How many of those promises have you kept?

A UNIVERSAL TRUTH

If you didn't fare too well, don't be too hard on yourself! Remember, a universal truth about all of us is that we are imperfect. This does not mean we shouldn't stretch ourselves to improve, and it certainly doesn't mean that we're hopeless. It does mean, however, that we share a common trait with everyone around us: imperfection. If we don't confess or identify this imperfection to ourselves, that lack of honesty alone can be the biggest and most harmful lie we will ever tell.

I would propose that *bad guys* don't care whether they improve or not. Most *bad guys* will continue pretending to themselves that they are really *good guys*, because they won't identify the imperfections in their character. They have already chosen the path of least resistance, caving to their bad nature and fooling themselves into thinking they are *good guys*.

Good guys, on the other hand, don't like these imperfections. They want to improve. They want to live with integrity. They push themselves, sometimes uncomfortably so, to be honest with themselves and to trust themselves. Exploring our imperfections by reflecting on how we treat ourselves or lie to ourselves is an avenue that requires true candor and humility. Recognizing that we truly are flawed and no better than anyone else is true humility.

BE STRAIGHT WITH YOURSELF ABOUT WHAT MATTERS

This may start off like one of those Dr. Seuss chapters. You know, "Be who you are and say what you feel, because those who mind don't matter and those who matter don't mind." Well, that is the concept, sort of. Be straight with yourself about what matters, and what matters most is being honest with yourself.

We've discussed self-awareness in previous chapters. Now is the time for self-awareness about our own behaviors toward ourselves. Just as with others we deem trustworthy, we will trust ourselves more if we can admit that we don't always keep promises to ourselves, rather than making excuses for why we don't keep those promises. It's time to develop a greater awareness of the valid trust relationship we have with ourselves, not the counterfeit one we may create that allows us to continue to fool ourselves: to *save face*. In earlier chapters we discussed ways we let others fool us; well, we let ourselves fool us, too. Just as with others, if we aren't totally honest with ourselves in this personal assessment, yet another bad guy is fooling us. This time, the bad guy is the person you see in the mirror.

We can become honest with ourselves by better managing our mental scripts (that voice in our heads that is constantly pestering us). One of the best books I've read on the topic of managing our mental scripts is *The Untethered Soul* by Michael Singer.[1] In this book, Singer walks us through our relationship with the inner voice of our mental script and discusses ways we can learn to better manage our mental scripts to be more honest and trustworthy to ourselves. He asks if we would we be friends with someone who talked to us the way our mental script talks to us: "Would we be friends with someone who constantly lies to us the way our mental script lies to us?" Singer suggests we think of our mental script as a possible roommate. Would we like this roommate or would we be searching for a new one?

From the perspective of *Trust Rules*, I might ask, "How do you get along with your roommate, your inner voice? Is the roommate a *good guy* or a *bad guy*?"

We've learned the importance of honesty in our trusted relationships with others. We trust those who are honest with us. We trust those who don't ignore us when we are behaving badly but tell us about that bad behavior. We trust those who give us candid feedback. This is what we must do for *ourselves*. Be that good guy to yourself. Examine your intrapersonal integrity and work toward telling yourself the truth about your behaviors toward *you*. Clean up that mental script.

CLEAN UP YOUR MENTAL SCRIPT

We need to use some mental floss to clean up the cluttered corners of our minds, where we've stored all those good intentions or broken promises to ourselves, or even our assessment of what is good. While we may have tucked these promises away in some corner of our minds, they are there, subconsciously reminding us that we can't trust ourselves. These broken promises to ourselves create *clutter* that won't let us see a better and more self-trusting person.

Think of the problem as a room *full* of clutter. Sometimes a room can be filled with so much litter that you can't even see the true color of the rug or hardwood floor. It isn't until you remove the mess that you can finally see the true condition of the floor. After you remove the disorder, you may notice that the floor is scratched here and there and needs some repair, but until you removed that clutter, you had no idea that the floor needed some work to make it better.

The same is true with us. We have to remove the mess so we can see the scratches and accurately assess how to build a more self-trusting nature. The clutter acts as a buffer between us and the self-trusting person we can become.

Singer asks, "Do you see that you have built, and struggle to maintain, a very specific concept of who you are and how others should view you?" He agrees the most important and valuable concept of who you are is who *you* think you are!

WAYS YOU MIGHT MISTREAT YOURSELF

Let's consider ways in which you might behave in untrustworthy ways toward yourself. Suppose that on a Sunday night you tell yourself that this coming week you are going to start treating yourself better by not working such long, hard hours. You are going to leave the office by 6:00 every night. You've reflected on your work situation and realized that overwork has just become a bad habit. You are putting everyone else's desires, projects, and commitments at work ahead of your own. You are exhausted, irritable, feeling overworked and underappreciated. You realize you would be more effective if you were able to distance yourself somewhat from your work environment. You've made the rational decision that it will be far better for you and your workplace if you can better manage your work/life situation. Monday morning comes and you stay committed to the promise you made to yourself the previous evening.

At 5:45 the next afternoon, however, a colleague dashes into your office and requests you review the presentation he has prepared for tomorrow's 8:00 A.M. team meeting. It's clear your colleague expects you will do so; you've always been responsive to his requests. And because of your obsessive commitment to quality work, you are his favorite colleague. What do you do?

If you say, "Yes," you may make your colleague happy. This will also reinforce that he can trust that you will help him out when he is in a pinch. Being a *good guy* in your relationship with your colleague, however, will let yourself down. You will break the commitment you made to yourself, making you a *bad guy* to yourself. You are the one, however, who set up the expectation that your colleague could trust you to help him out in a pinch. What do you do? It's not an easy decision. It's up to each one of us to decide, but this chapter is about including yourself, and trust for yourself, in that equation.

In another instance, imagine that you decide, when Monday arrives, that you will begin a healthy eating and exercise program. Then Monday arrives and leaves you behind. Monday evening, you're invited to dinner at a friend's home. It's your friend's signature dish but not a healthy choice. You don't want to disappoint her, so you eat and drink and rationalize your behavior as an exception. You'll keep that promise you made to yourself, *tomorrow.*

Tomorrow comes and you have a client lunch meeting. They choose a burger place. Once again, you don't go on that program and continue to eat poorly. Next Monday comes, and you try again, but your colleagues invite you to lunch to celebrate the successful advertising campaign of your biggest client. You skip that walk you were going to take on your lunch hour and celebrate with bad food choices. This becomes your predictable pattern.

What is happening that might be even more important than that healthy lifestyle change you may want to make? You are being untrustworthy to yourself. You have lied to yourself about what you are going to do, and you might be getting into a habit of repeatedly rationalizing away the lies (just this once, I'll *really* start next week, I didn't really mean that I'd eat totally healthy, etc.) over and over.

COLD TURKEY

In the first work example, it might not be fair to cut your colleague off cold turkey. It might have been more prudent for you to inform your colleagues that, starting next Monday, you will be leaving work by 6:00 each night. Despite your promise to yourself, you still want to help—so, if they have work that needs to be reviewed, you will be glad to help them out, *if* they can get material to you earlier in the day. Out of respect to yourself, at 6:00 P.M. you are walking out the door. Emergencies and unexpected problems may occur, and you may have to alter your behavior once in a while, but most of those emergencies probably could have been handled earlier in the day or handled before they became emergencies. The problem is that you're reacting to their schedule, not yours. Remember, you've rationally reviewed your workday and made the decision that you *and* your workplace will be better off if you develop a better balance between your work and your life.

In the second instance, where you've promised yourself to take better care of yourself by exercising and eating better, the same is also true.

AN ANALOGY: DO YOU TRUST SOMEONE WHO LIES TO YOU?

How much do you trust someone who openly lies to you not once, but over and over again? Michael Josephson, from The Josephson Institute of Ethics, asks: "Just how many times does someone have to lie to you before you call them a liar?"

How many of us would have to call *ourselves* liars because we lie to ourselves so freely? It may seem harmless to lie to yourself. Doesn't it, however, develop a predictable behavior over time that soon defines how much you can trust yourself or how much self-confidence you have?

Telling a friend that you have committed to yourself to leave work at 6:00 P.M. and then committing to your own promise can start a ground swell of self-confidence and self-trust that will build upon itself. Meeting your own promises, no matter how small, may start a virtuous cycle of self-trust that might eventually make the really big issues clearer and easier for you and turn a difficult decision from gray to black or white for you.

Could you have a healthy, positive relationship with a person who lied to you again and again? Would you continue to trust that this person would not lie the next time he or she made a promise or commitment to you? Probably not. Similarly, when you make promises to yourself about something you will or won't do, but then do not follow through, you learn not to trust yourself. You, in essence, build an untrustworthy relationship with yourself, making you a *bad guy* to yourself. Strange, but it happens all too frequently. Self-reflection, personal honesty, staying true to what you think is right for you, and following through on promises you make to yourself can break this habit.

A SECOND CHANCE?

Will you give yourself a second chance (or third or fourth or . . .)? To alter this untrustworthy relationship with yourself, your actions have to begin to match your words. In an earlier chapter, Doug Conant, former CEO of Campbell Soup Inc., told us that when we are trying to mend a relationship gone awry, we have to *behave* our way back into a trustworthy relationship. The same is true of the relationship we have with ourselves. To learn to trust ourselves again, we have to be honest and trustworthy *to* ourselves, as measured by our actions and behaviors, not words or intentions.

The most important relationship we will ever have is with ourselves. Value that relationship with yourself as much as you value the relationship with your most trusted confidant. Become a good guy to yourself!

As the epigram at the beginning of this chapter notes, "This above all: to thine own self be true. And it must follow, as the night the day, thou canst not then be false to any man."

Shakespeare seems to have known quite a bit about sorting good guys from bad guys too, didn't he? Of course, he borrowed this saying from words inscribed above the Oracle at Delphi. Even by then, it had stood the test of time.

Bob Eckert, Chairman Emeritus of the Board, Mattel Inc., in agreement with the importance of self-trust, told me, "The ultimate test of trust is with myself."

Eckert believes that to be able to trust others, you have to first know you can trust yourself. For example, can you trust yourself to keep a secret, if someone asks that you do? This act not only shows trust to the person who told you the secret, but shows *you* that you are a trustworthy person, as well. Eckert explains that, if he says to someone, "*This is between you and me,*" he will go to his grave with that secret. For Eckert, it's all about personal integrity and understanding the importance of that integrity to our lives and our relationships, those relationships with others and the all-important relationship we have with ourselves.

SO, ONCE WE'VE MADE THAT COMMITMENT TO OURSELVES, WHAT HAPPENS?

When our actions match the words and thoughts we tell ourselves, we begin to know we can handle whatever life throws our way. We begin to worry less about what *might* happen, about what untrustworthy people (*bad guys*) might do to us. We know that life is imperfect, and we gain confidence in our ability and capability to deal with any *bad* we encounter in our lives. Trusting ourselves allows us to enjoy life, feel positive about life, and have greater peace of mind. Trusting ourselves also allows us to let go of worry and concern, because when we are capable of managing ourselves, we develop confidence we can also manage the other relationships in our lives. The result is that we also begin to be more willing to trust others (those that deserve our trust, that is!). We begin to achieve peace of mind. The importance is that we align our thoughts, words, and actions!

Now that we've gained greater insight into the importance of trusting ourselves, we've conquered the gamut of trust and the rules that separate the good guys from the bad guys in work and life. We have amassed a tremendous amount of information. In the final chapter, I'll conclude with some words about trust and its importance to our successful and happy lives.

NOTE

1.   Michael A. Singer, *The Untethered Soul* (Oakland: New Harbinger and Noetic Books, 2007).

Chapter 22

Final Thoughts about Trust
in Our Lives

Love all, trust a few, do wrong to none.

—William Shakespeare

WHOM TO TRUST? Whom not to trust? When to trust? When not to trust? These are likely among the most important decisions we will ever make. After reading this book, perhaps you'll realize, as I did, that you've got some work ahead of you. The Trust Rules Toolkit can be that provocative catalyst to get you thinking and talking about the importance of trusted relationships to your lives and in making those important trust decisions.

Below, I've tried to summarize a few of the important concepts from this book. You will want to return to these often.

CONTINUE TO RE-EVALUATE

We should re-evaluate our relationships often. In fact, we should reassess our inner circle of confidants on a regular basis. It's impossible to be 100 percent trustworthy every day of our lives, but we should try to spend time with people who wear the trustworthy hat more often than not. In the business world, doing so can mean the difference between having effective relationships that lead to improved performance and having a contingent of solo artists who can't advance a common cause. In our personal lives, choosing someone to include in our inner circle of confidants, based on the insights from this book, can increase our probability of success, peacefulness, and happiness.

DO THEY MEASURE UP?

One goal of this book has been to encourage us to reflect on those people we have placed in our innermost circle of family, friends, and intimate confidants and see how they measure up as truly trustworthy people. Our good judgment in letting them into our innermost circle in the first place may be validated or some red flags may go up that force us to rethink our choices. Either way, I hope this book is a useful tool you can employ throughout your life.

It's easy to tell the really good guys out there; they rarely let us down. They never do things that are harmful to us—even if they would personally benefit in some way by doing so. We ask them to do something, they do it. We call them, they return our calls; we need them, and they are there. Even when we don't ask them to do something, they somehow know we need them. We can just always count on them to help us and never do harm to us. They *really* do have our backs.

It's also easy to tell the really bad guys. But it's the bad guys that *sometimes* look like good guys that can wreck our work and personal lives. When someone we've thought was a good guy really lets us down, it's the worst case of all. As one of my interviewees put it:

It's OK If Some People Are Jerks

When you meet someone for the first time and they prove to be a jerk, I'm fine with that. It's the people you believe to be real, good, and people of integrity, that turn out to be jerks that break your heart.

—Patricia Clay, Actress

Hopefully, the Trust Rules Toolkit will now help us better assess just who those bad guys are. Remember, though, most of us are guilty of making way too many excuses for the bad behaviors of those who are important to us, especially in our personal lives. In doing so, we overlook critical signals that could help us better manage our personal lives the same way we would in the workplace. We frequently overlook key signals that could prevent us from being hurt by those who exhibit bad behaviors.

Many of us have experienced situations when we found out we'd misperceived what we thought was a good relationship. Most of all, we fooled ourselves. We let our emotions allow us to believe that, contrary to the evidence in front of us, someone would behave differently with us than with others. The day came, however, when our relationship changed and we were no longer able to defend this person's bad behavior, and we realized instead that we'd been a victim of it.

I cannot begin to count the number of people who have come into my office or into my life, devastated by the actions or behaviors of someone they had trusted. Their faces wear that look that says they just can't make it through the day. They are burdened by humiliation and stunned that they could have been duped so badly. These situations encouraged me to learn more about assessing trustworthiness in others and to help others make better trust-related decisions.

Now that I've thought about trust so much and its impact on family, country, and community, I wonder if we haven't taken denial to extreme limits.

HAVE WE GONE TOO FAR?

Have we gone too far by not differentiating good guys from bad guys in our lives?

- In our school systems, are we more concerned about protecting the rights of the bully instead of protecting the ones bullied? Or is it just that parents and teachers do not notice the problem?

- In our workplaces, is the whistle-blower often considered the bad guy?

- In our political system, are we all too quick to reelect those who have exhibited abominable behaviors that should have sent a message that they should never be trusted with our country's welfare?

- In our criminal system, are we more concerned about protecting the rights of the criminal than we are about protecting the rights of the person being harmed?

- In our religious affiliations, in ways that defy belief, the Catholic Church protected the rights of priests who harmed young children, while the children were left on their own to live lives of secret shame.

- In our family systems, do we no longer show dismay to those who willingly lie to their families, while they engage in trysts that satisfy their ego, yet immeasurably harm the psyches of their children and spouse/partner? Such actions break the bonds of trust and can be impediments to healthy personal and family development.

Philosophers warn us that, when basic trust is not present, a society is on the verge of collapse. We only have to read the morning newspaper or watch the morning news to start off the day with multiple mental pictures of deceit, lies, and selfish behaviors that mark our nation. It is time to reestablish trust in our own lives and, by extension, in the lives of our communities and our nation.

Here's a pertinent quote from Dave Weiner, Founder and CEO, Marketing Support Inc., and Author:

WE ALL HAVE OUR MOMENTS

None of us is "all good"; we all have our moments. If we go back to one of my earlier books, *Power Freaks*, and look at the characteristics of a white-collar psychopath, we are pretty close to defining who is bad. On the other hand, John Wayne Gacy, a model for antisocial personality disorder and psychopathy, was the president of his Junior Chamber of Commerce and dressed as a clown to entertain kids at a Shriners hospital.

People who are simply nasty and mean and reflect psychopathic traits are easier to detect because they let it all hang out. It's those who seem to be normal, but are capable of doing great harm to us, that are often the difficult ones to detect. Psychopaths, particularly the secondary or white-collar ones, can hide everything behind what Hervey Cleckley, the early authority on the subject, called "The Mask of Sanity."

—Dave Weiner, Founder and CEO, Marketing Support Inc., and Author

LET'S REWARD THE GOOD GUYS

All people aren't the same. Greater rewards *should* go to those who are good guys. Then the rest of us will know how to behave to get those same rewards (not just financial rewards, but rewards of peace of mind, social acceptance, love, and respect of our friends and families). It's a basic principle of human development that we repeat behaviors for which we are rewarded and not punished. We often learn these principles from observing how others are rewarded and punished.

I'm not judging how the bad guys got there or whether they deserve my help or others' help in some way, or whether I should be kind to bad guys as well as good guys. I don't think the differentiation has anything to do with race, religion, gender, age, sexual preference, income, or any other demographic characteristics. I'm merely saying that some people are better guys than others. I don't plan on being unkind to the bad guys; I just want to learn how to keep them out of my inner circle and yours.

I've taught organizational behavior to graduate students for many years. The very basis of that course is that, in the workplace, we should reward those who exhibit behaviors we want them to repeat. It's good to discriminate, not by demographic characteristics, but by behaviors. Those who work harder, accomplish more, and create more value in the workplace SHOULD be rewarded more. There's a great analogy with trust: Those who are more trustworthy, those who are people of integrity, should become part of our inner circle of confidants. Those who exhibit behaviors that show they are untrustworthy should not!

A COMPETITIVE ADVANTAGE

Research has shown that, when companies create cultures of trust, they have a competitive advantage. Robert Hurley, Professor of Management at Fordham University, asks why anyone would want to stay in a stressful, untrusting workplace culture, if they have a better choice. Surely, the same is true of our family and personal lives.

There seems to be little or no argument for creating family/friendship/workplace cultures that are not of a trusting nature. Our families can certainly also have a *competitive advantage* if we create family cultures with foundations built on trust. Not all marriages or partnerships are able to last forever, but the way they come apart has huge implications for the development of trust with our children, grandchildren, school systems, communities, and society at large.

Some may worry that building an inner circle of good guys will turn us all into wimps, people not *tough* enough to deal with *real* life. But being a good guy doesn't mean you are a wimp. Good guys also can be driven, committed, innovative, tough, and disciplined at what they do. For example, when CEO Denny Brown was asked how he searches for the good guys in work and life, he replied:

The Good Guys Wear the White Hats

That's easy, the good guys wear the white hats and the bad guys wear the black hats. But seriously, I think we can be a fierce and shrewd competitor and still be honest, caring, kind, and thoughtful, etc. This kind of business and person will ultimately be the most successful in the work place and life in general.

—Denny L. Brown, Founder, CEO, Linden Associates

BEWARE OF THE CHARMER

If there is only one lesson, idea, or concept we can take away from this book, it's not to make excuses for the bad behavior of others. In many instances, egregious acts of betrayal are preceded by a series of bad behaviors for which we made excuses.

Many of us are still swayed by what someone says, rather than by that person's actions. And it's easier for us to not really examine these actions, especially if we are benefiting in some way from their misdeeds. Those con artists (pseudo good guys) can convince us through their words that their actions did not mean what our eyes saw (just because I lied to my boss, wife, or coworker doesn't mean I would ever lie to you). If we are swayed by words, instead of actions, we have only ourselves to blame. Beware of the charmer!

AVERAGE GUYS

I've learned that good guys are few and far between. *Average* guys abound in the world. They may look like good guys at times when their lives are going well, but those that are truly honorable and filled with integrity are rare. I've had the honor of knowing a few of these good guys; I hope you have, too.

The truth is that most of us live and work with some pretty *average* guys, not good guys or bad buys, but *average* guys. Thus, this book and the Trust Rules Toolkit help us learn how to live, work, and carry on our lives with the average guy, the *guy* who may have a lot of *conditions* under which he/she can be trustworthy. Thus, we have to learn to recognize the conditions or situations under which the average guy will sway one way or the other. Knowledge is power. Knowing and understanding the *average* guys and being better able to predict their trustworthy behavior is a key factor to our sense of effective, efficient, and peaceful lives.

We hopefully have learned how to forgive the mistakes and shortcomings of these average guys (who knows, we might be one ourselves!), how to cope when we've been betrayed, how to decide if an *average* guy is worth reconciling with in our work or personal lives, and how to live and work with those who aren't trustworthy.

We've discovered that sometimes *we're* the bad guys to others and to ourselves. Perhaps we are just *average* guys, too. That's a really easy insight to overlook. Now that we know this, as we move forward, we hope we have learned from our past mistakes. We know we are going to make new mistakes, but we just don't want to keep making the *same* mistakes. Hopefully, we're now wise enough to know when we've done so and make appropriate amends.

Maybe most importantly, we've also learned we should never forget the influence others have on our thinking. Each of us can be swayed, if only slightly, by those we spend time with. This book has cautioned us to associate and spend our time with the good guys. For many of us, this creates a trust dilemma.

A TRUST DILEMMA

The Golden Rule reminds us to treat others as we would want to be treated. The reality is that many of us grow up, perform the *good guy vs. bad guy* calculation, and decide that we need to cut some people out of our lives. We recognize that dismissing or ignoring the bad guys is actually quite healthy and contributes to our overall happiness. So, how do we juggle that internal conflict?

I want to be known as a kind, fair person. I also know that if I am not kind and fair to people I've identified as bad guys, how can I really be a good guy? Conceivably, it doesn't mean we will be unkind or thoughtless to those bad guys. We just don't want them in our inner circle!

An interview with New York Supreme Court Justice Joseph McGuire expanded on this. He helped me make the distinction. Justice McGuire noted that when he was first elected to the New York State Supreme Court bench, he was told that he was to do *justice* and not to *judge*.

That's what I want to do: be just, but not judge.

PERHAPS GOOD GUYS VS. BAD GUYS IS OVERLY SIMPLISTIC

The distinction between good guys and bad guys I've created for this book is symbolic in nature. Most of us fall along a continuum of good and bad behaviors.

Aristotle would say that the difference between good and bad people isn't that the bad guys are really bad; rather, they are short-term, immature thinkers who are unable to defer gratification for longer-term success and happiness.[1] Perhaps, Dr. David Harrison says it best:

The Best Guys

For me, the fundamental premise is that there are no good guys and no bad guys. There are people in organizations and in life who are more (or less) self-interested, rather than other-directed, more (or less) irresponsible or undependable, and more (or less) likely to show hostility, when they feel frustrated. I will tend to avoid those who are more of the above, but I can't shun them completely. The "best guys," the heroes, the members of the dance band on the Titanic, will give up themselves and do whatever is necessary for the people who depend on them.

—Professor Dave Harrison, Smeal College of Business Administration, The Pennsylvania State University

MORE FINAL THOUGHTS

Trust may not be as static a concept as I had thought in my earlier years. Instead, trust is a dynamic phenomenon, changing as experiences and life change us. I went into this research curious about how to differentiate someone I can trust from someone I can't trust. I've learned that trust can be fleeting in some people and that life's experiences test people in different ways. This is true for us as well . . . . Remember a time when you didn't feel so great, or you were in the midst of some crisis in your life? Don't you agree that you weren't as trustworthy to your friends and family as you would like to have been during that time?

Basically, however, regardless of any personal crises, we can be assured that the more negative characteristics people have, the more we want to steer clear of them.

Whether we are a CEO of a major multinational company trying to figure out whom we can trust to give us important strategic advice, a mom or dad trying to make friends with other parents in the school/parent organization, or a teenager trying to figure out how to get through adolescence, the formula is the same. If we want to be better people and enjoy our lives more fully, we must carefully guard whom we let into our inner circle of friends, coworkers, and family. This decision is the most important life decision we will ever make. Once we decide, we must never be afraid to reevaluate our decisions and reassess these decisions on a regular basis throughout our lives.

It is my sincere hope you will find the information in this book and the Trust Rules Toolkit a useful companion on this journey—a companion that helps you sort those good guys from the bad guys in *your* work and personal life.

NOTE

1. James O'Toole, *Applying Aristotle's Wisdom to Find Meaning and Happiness* (Stuttgart: Holtzbrinck Publishers, 2005).

Appendix

The Trust Rules Toolkit*

*If you choose to, you can print copies of these tables and use them to assess the trustworthiness of your current and potential confidants; use the self-directed tables to measure your own trustworthiness as well. Use the Stroh Family Board Meeting Agenda form for your very own monthly family board meetings.

Figure 6.1 Propensity to Trust Scale

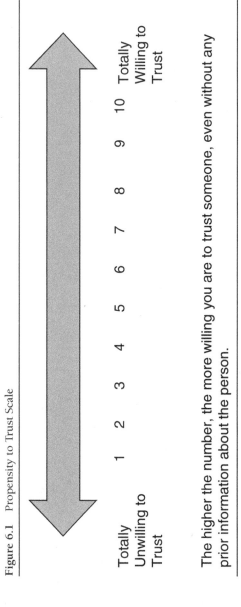

Totally
Unwilling to
Trust

1   2   3   4   5   6   7   8   9   10 Totally
                                        Willing to
                                        Trust

The higher the number, the more willing you are to trust someone, even without any prior information about the person.

Table 9.1 Trust Rules Questionnaire

Select a potential or current confidant. Respond to each questionnaire on a scale of 1-10, with 1 indicating the person **does not** have this characteristic and 10 meaning this person **does have** this characteristic. Place the number you have selected in the space provided at the beginning of each question. The sum of the numbers is the Total Score. The higher the number, the more trustworthy you perceive this person to be.

Value	Trait	Definitely Does Not Have Characteristic									Definitely Has Characteristic
___	This person has a history that demonstrates good values.	1	2	3	4	5	6	7	8	9	10
___	This person is likely to respond in a healthy way, when things go wrong.	1	2	3	4	5	6	7	8	9	10
___	This person admits and learns from mistakes.	1	2	3	4	5	6	7	8	9	10
___	This person has a self-awareness of how his/her behavior affects others.	1	2	3	4	5	6	7	8	9	10
___	This person treats everyone the same, regardless of level in the hierarchy (work or social).	1	2	3	4	5	6	7	8	9	10
___	This person demonstrates consistent good behavior.	1	2	3	4	5	6	7	8	9	10
___	This person has positive qualities, other than just good looks, a good education, and wealth.	1	2	3	4	5	6	7	8	9	10
___	This person never takes advantage of others with his/her own good looks, education, or wealth.	1	2	3	4	5	6	7	8	9	10
___	This person admits when he/she doesn't know something.	1	2	3	4	5	6	7	8	9	10
___	This person demonstrates absolute integrity.	1	2	3	4	5	6	7	8	9	10
___	This person genuinely considers others in his/her life.	1	2	3	4	5	6	7	8	9	10
___	This person voluntarily, in useful ways, tells me when I do something wrong.	1	2	3	4	5	6	7	8	9	10
___	This person helps me to be a better person.	1	2	3	4	5	6	7	8	9	10
___	I would introduce this person to my family and other trusted confidants.	1	2	3	4	5	6	7	8	9	10
___	This person responds in a healthy way, when he/she doesn't get his/her way.	1	2	3	4	5	6	7	8	9	10
___	This person holds him/herself to the same standards he/she established for others.	1	2	3	4	5	6	7	8	9	10
___	This person does the right thing.	1	2	3	4	5	6	7	8	9	10
___	This person sticks by others in bad/tough times.	1	2	3	4	5	6	7	8	9	10
___	This person speaks the same of everyone, whether in their presence or not.	1	2	3	4	5	6	7	8	9	10
___	This person is likely to share resources (time, space, money, friends).	1	2	3	4	5	6	7	8	9	10

___ **TOTAL SCORE (Total possible score between 20 and 200)**

Figure 9.1 Trust Rules Scale

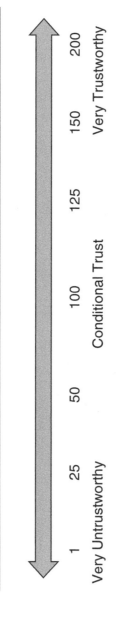

| 1 | 25 | 50 | 100 | 125 | 150 | 200 |

Very Untrustworthy   Conditional Trust   Very Trustworthy

Based on the Total Score from the Trust Rules Questionnaire, place your current or potential confidant on the Trust Rules Scale. The more positive characteristics, and the higher the number on the Trust Rules Questionnaire, the more you can trust this person.

Table 20.1 Trust Rules Self-Questionnaire

Answer each question by rating yourself on a scale of 1–10, 1 meaning you **do not** have this characteristic and 10 meaning you do have this characteristic. Place your rating on the space provided at the beginning of each question. Add each rating to get the Total Score. The higher the number, the more trustworthy you perceive yourself to be.

Value	Trait	I Definitely Do Not Have This Characteristic									I Definitely Have This Characteristic
___	Do you have a history that demonstrates good values?	1	2	3	4	5	6	7	8	9	10
___	Are you likely to respond in a healthy way, when things go wrong?	1	2	3	4	5	6	7	8	9	10
___	Do you admit and learn from mistakes?	1	2	3	4	5	6	7	8	9	10
___	Do you have a self-awareness that demonstrates you know how your behavior affects others?	1	2	3	4	5	6	7	8	9	10
___	Do you treat everyone the same, regardless of their level in the hierarchy (work or social)?	1	2	3	4	5	6	7	8	9	10
___	Do you demonstrate consistent good behaviors?	1	2	3	4	5	6	7	8	9	10
___	Do you have positive qualities, other than good looks, a good education, and wealth?	1	2	3	4	5	6	7	8	9	10
___	Do you never take advantage of others using your own good looks, education, or wealth?	1	2	3	4	5	6	7	8	9	10
___	Do you admit when you don't know something?	1	2	3	4	5	6	7	8	9	10
___	Do you demonstrate absolute integrity?	1	2	3	4	5	6	7	8	9	10
___	Do you genuinely consider others in your life?	1	2	3	4	5	6	7	8	9	10
___	Do you voluntarily, in healthy ways, tell others when they are doing something wrong?	1	2	3	4	5	6	7	8	9	10
___	Do you help others be better people?	1	2	3	4	5	6	7	8	9	10
___	Would others introduce you to their family and other trusted confidants?	1	2	3	4	5	6	7	8	9	10
___	Are you likely to respond in a healthy way, when you don't get your way?	1	2	3	4	5	6	7	8	9	10
___	Do you hold yourself to the same standards you establish for others?	1	2	3	4	5	6	7	8	9	10
___	Do you do the right thing?	1	2	3	4	5	6	7	8	9	10
___	Do you stick by others in bad/tough times?	1	2	3	4	5	6	7	8	9	10
___	Do you speak the same of people, whether they are in your presence or not?	1	2	3	4	5	6	7	8	9	10
___	Are you likely to share resources (time, space, money, friends)?	1	2	3	4	5	6	7	8	9	10

___ **TOTAL SCORE (Total possible score between 20 and 200)**

Figure 20.1   How Trustworthy Are You Scale

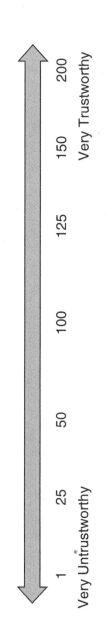

| 1 | 25 | 50 | 100 | 125 | 150 | 200 |

Very Untrustworthy

Very Trustworthy

Based on your Total Score from the Trust Rules Self-Questionnaire, place yourself on the Trust Rules Self-Scale. The higher the number, the more trustworthy you perceive yourself to be.

Stroh Family Board Meeting Agenda

Goal: Ensure that we are living *conscious lives*, where we know the *impact of our actions*, where we *own our paths* through life and take *responsibility for our own happiness*.

Exercises:

1. What went right or was amazing for me in the past month? _____
    _____

2. Everyone takes turns:
    "I like, I wish, I wonder"
    a) I like _____
    b) I wish _____
    c) I wonder _____
    "Happy, worried, frustrated"
    a) I am happy about _____
    b) I am worried about _____
    c) I am frustrated about _____

3. Reflection and Planning:
    How we spend our free time:
    • The things that I spent my free time on in the last month are:
    {are these things we are proud to be a part of, that we are developing with and that make us and/or the world better?}
    • Who am I spending my free time with:
    {are these people that we are proud to associate with, that make us and/or the world better?}

4. What did I do to make the world a better place this month:
    _____

5. My Goals:
    My top three goals for the next month are to:
    1.
    2.
    3.
    {report back on how did on my goals for the past month}

6.   You Give Me 3 Goals:

     Everyone in the family gives each other a goal to work on over the next month:

     1.   _____

     2.   _____

     3.   _____

     {how did I do on the goals you gave me for the past month}

7.   Am I happy? If not, what can I change to make myself happier:
     _____

8.   Optional:

     Share a:
     - Poem
     - Picture
     - Book you read
     - Painting
     - Thought or observation
     - Something from nature

9.   Monthly Optional Discussion Topics:
     - Science report about something we are interested in
     - Define our family values
     - Assess our family's impact on our environment
     - Find a service-learning topic that we want to get involved in supporting, to help less blessed people or things on the planet
     - Read a book together
     - Invite a guest speaker (Auntie Angie & Uncle Joey?)
     - Share a hug

Bibliography

Ablow, Keith. 2007. *Living the Truth: Transform Your Life Through the Power of Insight and Honesty.* New York: Little Brown & Company.

Arris, S., Aimee A. Cole-Laramore, and N. Nykodym. 2002. "Trust and Technology in the Virtual Organization." *SAM Advanced Management Journal* 67.

Atkinson, S., and D. Butcher. 2003. "Trust in the Context of Management Relationships: An Empirical Study." *SAM Advanced Management Journal* 68.

Berman, Jason J., Robert D. Costigan, and Selim S. Ilter. 1998. "A Multi-Dimensional Study of Trust in Organizations." *Journal of Managerial Issues* 10.

Blow, Adrian, J., and Kelly Hartnett. 2005. "Infidelity in Committed Relationships II: A Substantive Review." *Journal of Marital and Family Therapy* 31, no. 2: 217–233.

Bodhi, Bhikkhu. 2007. *Association with the Wise.* Buddhist Publication Society, http://wanderling.tripod.com/wise.html, March 1.

Bohnet, Iris, and Richard Zeckhauser. 2004. "Trust, Risk and Betrayal." *Journal of Economic Behavior & Organization* 55: 467–84.

CBS *Sunday Morning.* 2014. *100 Best Companies to Work For.* August 31.

Cohen, Randy. 2004. *The Good, the Bad, and the Difference.* New York: Broadway Books.

Costigan, Robert D., Selim S. Itler, Richard C. Insinga, G. Kranas, and Vladimir A. Kureshov. 2003. "Predictors of Employee Trust of Their CEO: A Three-Country Study." *Journal of Management Issues*, XVI, no. 2: 197–216.

Covey, Stephen, R. 2006. *The Speed of Trust.* New York: Free Press.

Cox, Susie R., Rebecca J. Bennett, Thomas M. Tripp, and Karl Aquino. 2012. "An Empirical Test of Forgiveness Motives' Effects on Employees' Health and Well-being." *Journal of Occupational Health Psychology*, 17(3): 330–340.

DeSteno, David. 2014. "Who Can You Trust." *Harvard Business Review*: March.

Driver, J., A. Tabares, A. Shapiro, E. Y. Nahm, and J. Gottman. 2003. "Interactional Patterns in Marital Success or Failure: Gottman Laboratory Studies." Pp. 493–513 in F. Walsh, ed., *Normal Family Process: Growing Diversity and Complexity.* New York: Guilford.

Dunn, Jennifer R., and Maurice E. Schweitzer. 2005. "Feeling and Believing: The Influence of Emotion on Trust." *Journal of Personality and Social Psychology* 88, no. 5: 736–48.

Dutton, Jane, and Belle Rose Ragins. 2007. *Exploring Positive Relationships at Work.* New Jersey: Lawrence Erlbaum Associates.

Ellis, K., and P. Shockley-Zalabak. 2001. "Trust in Top Management and Immediate Supervisor: The Relationship to Satisfaction, Perceived Organizational Effectiveness, and Information Receiving." *Communication Quarterly* 49.

Feldman, Robert. 2009. *The Liar in Your Life: The Way to Truthful Relationships*. U.S. Edition: Twelve.

Feng, Jinjuan, Jonathan Lazar, and Jenny Preece. 2004. "Empathy and Online Interpersonal Trust: A Fragile Relationship." *Behavior & Information Technology* 23, no. 2: 97–106.

Friend, Celeste M. 2001. "Trust and the Presumption of Translucency." *Social Theory and Practice* 27.

Fukuyama, Francis. 1995. *Trust*. New York: The Free Press.

Galford, Robert, and Anne Seibold Drapeau. 2003. "The Enemies of Trust." *Harvard Business Review*, February.

George, Bill, Peter Sims, Andrew McLean, and Diana Mayer. 2007. *Discovering Your Authentic Leadership. Harvard Business Review* (February).

Gill, Harjinder, Kathleen Boies, Joan E. Finegan, and Jeffrey McNally. 2005. "Antecedents of Trust: Establishing a Boundary Condition for the Relation Between Propensity to Trust and Intention to Trust." *Journal of Business and Psychology* 19, no. 3: 287–302.

Gini, Al. 2006. *Why It's Hard to Be Good*. New York: Routledge.

Gladwell, Malcolm. 2007. *The Tipping Point: How Little Things Can Make a Big Difference*. New York: Little Brown and Company.

Goffee, Robert, and Gareth Jones. 2005. "Managing Authenticity: The Paradox of Great Leadership." *Harvard Business Review* (December 1).

Gordon, Kristina Coop, Farrah M. Hughes, Nathan D. Tomcik, Lee J. Dixon, and Samantha C. Litzinger. 2009. "Widening Spheres of Impact: The Role of Forgiveness in Marital and Family Functioning." *Journal of Family Psychology*, 23(1), 1–13.

Govier, Trudy. 1998. *Dilemmas of Trust*. Montreal: McGill-Queen's University Press.

Grohol, John M. 2013. "How Common is Cheating and Infidelity?" *World of Psychology*, March 2.

Hamlin, Kiley J., and Karen Wynn. 2011. "Young Infants Prefer Prosocial to Antisocial Others." *Cognitive Development* 26(1): 30–39.

Hannon, Peggy A., Eli J. Finkel, Madoka Kumashiro, and Caryle E. Rusbult. 2012. "The Soothing Effects of Forgiveness on Victims' Perpetrators' Blood Pressure." *Personal Relationships* 19: 279–289.

Hardin, Russell. 2004. *Distrust*. New York: Russell Sage.

Heintzelman, Ashley, Nancy L. Murdock, Romana C. Krycak, and Larissa Seay. 2014. "Recovery From Infidelity: Differentiation of Self, Trauma, Forgiveness, and Post-traumatic Growth Among Couples in Continuing Relationships." *Couple and Family Psychology: Research and Practice* 3(1): 13–29.

Helmick, Raymond G., and Rodney L. Petersen. 2001. *Forgiveness and Reconciliation*. London: Templeton Foundation Press.

Holland, William. 2006. *Are There Any Good Jobs Left?* Westport: Praeger.

Hurley, Robert F. 2006. "The Decision to Trust." *Harvard Business Review*: September.

Kant, Immanuel. 1976. *Foundations of the Metaphysics of Morals*. Translated by Lewis White Beck. Indianapolis: Bubbs-Merril.

Kelly, Anita. 2012. Presentation, Session 3189, 12 to 12:50 P.M., Room W303C, Level III, Orange County Convention Center. *American Psychological Association's 120th annual convention*, Saturday, August 4.

Kidd, Celeste, Holly Palmeri, and Richard Aslin. 2013. "Rational Snacking: Young Children's Decision on the Marshmallow Task Is Moderated by Beliefs about Reliability." *Cognition* 126: 109–114.

Kim, Peter, Donald L. Ferrin, Cecily Cooper, and Kurt T. Dirks. 2004. "Removing the Shadow of Suspicion: The Effects of Apology vs. Denial for Repairing Competence vs. Integrity-based Trust Violations." *Journal of Applied Psychology* 89: 104–18.

Klein, Charles. 1995. *How to Forgive When You Can't Forget*. New York: Berkley Books.

Kramer, Roderick M. 1999. "Trust and Distrust in Organizations: Emerging Perspectives, Enduring Questions." *Annual Review of Psychology* 50.

Kramer, Roderick M., and Karen S. Cook., eds. 2004. *Trust and Distrust in Organizations: Dilemmas and Approaches*. New York: Russell Sage.

Lawler, Kathleen A., Jarred W. Younger, Rachel L. Piferi, Rebecca L. Jobe, Kimberly A. Edmondson, and Warren H. Jones. 2005. "The Unique Effects of Forgiveness on Health: An Exploration of Pathways." *Journal of Behavioral Medicine* 28(2):157–67.

Levine, Stuart R. 2007. *Cut to the Chases*. New York: Doubleday.

Lucas, Leyland M. 2005. "The Impact of Trust and Reputation on the Transfer of Best Practices." *Journal of Knowledge Management* 9, no. 4: 87–101.

Macoby, Michael. 1997. "Building Trust is an Art." *Research Technology Management* 40: 56–57.

Malhotra, D., and Keith J. Murnighan. 2002. "The Effects of Contracts on Interpersonal Trust." *Administrative Science Quarterly* 47.

Manktelow, James, and Amy Carlson. "Active Listening: Hear What People Are Really Saying." http://www.mindtools.com/CommSkll/ActiveListening.html.

Martin, Mirta M. 1998. "Trust Leadership." *Journal of Leadership Studies* 5.

Mayer, Roger, James Davis, and David Schoorman. 1995. "An Integration Model of Organizational Trust." *Academy of Management Review,* 20: 709.

Mischel, Walter, Ebbe B. Ebbesen, and Antonette Raskoff Zeiss. 1972. "Cognitive and Attentional Mechanisms in Delay of Gratification." *Journal of Personality and Social Psychology* 21: 204–218.

Mishra, Aneil, and Karen Mishra. 2013. *Becoming a Trustworthy Leader*. East Sussex: Routledge.

Neuman, J. H., and R. A. Baron. 2004. "Aggression in the Workplace: A Social-Psychological Perspective." Pp. 13–40 in S. Fox and P. E. Spector, ed., *Counterproductive Work Behavior: Investigations of Actors and Targets*. Washington, DC: APA Press.

Nelson, Mariah Burton. n. d. www.mariahburtonnelson.com/forgivework.htm.

O'Toole, James. 2005. *Applying Aristotle's Wisdom to Find Meaning and Happiness*. Holtzbrinck Publishers.

Pelucchi, Sara, Giorgia F. Paleari, Camillo Regalia, and Frank D. Fincham. 2013. "Self-Forgiveness in Romantic Relationships: It Matters to Both of Us." *Journal of Family Psychology* 27(4): 541–549.

Pratt, Michael, and Kurt Dirks. 2007. "Rebuilding Trust and Restoring Positive Relationships: A Commitment-Based View of Trust." Pp. 117–36 in Jane E. Dutton and Belle Rose Ragins, ed., *Exploring Positive Relationships at Work*. New Jersey: Lawrence Erlbaum Associates.

Reina, Dennis S., and Michelle L. Reina. 2006. *Trust and Betrayal in the Workplace*. San Francisco: Berrett-Koehler.

Roberts, Laura Morgan. 2007. "From Proving to Becoming: How Positive Relationships Create a Context for Self-Discovery and Self-Actualization." Pp. 29–45 in Jane Dutton and Belle Rose Ragins, ed., *Exploring Positive Relationships at Work: Building a Theoretical and Research Foundation*. New Jersey: Lawrence Erlbaum.

Robinson, Sandra L. 1996. "Trust and Breach of the Psychological Contract." *Administrative Science Quarterly* 41.

Ryan, M. J. 2004. *Trusting Yourself*. New York: Broadway Books.

Shafir, Rebecca Z. 2000. *The Zen of Listening*. Wheaton: Quest Books.

Shellenbarger, Sue. 2000. "Workplace Upheavals Seem to Be Eroding Employees' Trust." *The Wall Street Journal*, June 21, Work & Family Section.

Simon, Sidney B., and S. Suzanne Simon. 1990. *Forgiveness: How to Make Peace with Your Past and Get on With your Life*. New York: Warner Books.

Singer, Michael A. 2007. *The Untethered Soul*. Oakland: Co-published by New Harbinger and Noetic Books.

Snyder, Bill. 2015. *Gates Foundation CEO: Good Intentions Aren't Enough*. Insights by Stanford: January 23.

Spector, Michele D., and Gwen E. Jones. 2004. "Trust in the Workplace: Factors Affecting Trust Formation Between Team Members." *Journal of Social Psychology* 144, no. 3: 331–41.

Stoller, Gary. 2007. "Infidelity is in the Air for Road Warriors." *USAToday*: April 19.

Storey, Tim. 2010. *Comeback & Beyond: How to Turn Your Setback into Your Comeback*. Goshen: Harrison House.

Stroh, L. K., J. S. Black, M. E. Mendenhall, and H. B. Gregersen. 2005. *International Assignments: An Integration of Strategy, Research and Practice*. New Jersey: Lawrence Erlbaum Associate.

Stroh, L. K., G. Northcraft, and M. Neale. 2002. *Organizational Behavior: The Management Challenge*. New Jersey: Lawrence Erlbaum Associates.

Stroh, L., J. S. Black, H. B. Gregersen, and M. E. Mendenhall. 2005. *International Assignments: An Integration of Strategy, Research & Practice*. New York: Lawrence Erlbaum Associates.

Stroh, L., and Homer Johnson. 2006. *The Basic Principles of Effective Consulting*. New York: Lawrence Erlbaum Associates.

Teck-Hua, Ho, and Keith Weigelt. 2005. "Trust Building among Strangers." *Management Science* 51, no. 4: 519–30.

Theron, Sally. 2011. "Personality and Individual Differences." *Digit Ratio (2D:4D) and Individual Differences Research*: 51, (4), September, 423–428.

Toussaint, Lauren, Grant Shields, Gabriel Dorn, and George M. Slavich. 2014. "Effects of Lifetime Stress Exposure on Mental and Physical Health in Young Adulthood: How Stress Degrades and Forgiveness Protects Health." *Journal of Health Psychology*. August.

Tzafrir, Shay S., Gedaliahu H. Harel, Yehuda Baruch, and Shimon L. Dolan. 2004. "The Consequences of Emerging HRM Practices for Employees' Trust in their Managers." *Personnel Review* 33, no. 6: 628–47.

Warrell, Margie. 2013. "Why Leaders Must 'Get Real'—5 Ways to Unlock Authentic Leadership." *Forbes*: May 20.

Ysseldyk, Renate, and Michael J. A. Wohl. 2012. "I Forgive Therefore I'm Committed: A Longitudinal Examination of Commitment after a Romantic Relationship Transgression." *Journal of Behavioural Science/Revue* 44(4): 257–263.